Praise

'David's story is fascinating. It's such a big thing to move to another country and set up a business – from scratch – let alone one that is as successful as GoLocalise, and I take my hat off to him. Huge respect.

His passion for words and language oozes from every page of this book, but having had the pleasure of getting to know him, it seems clear to me that it is David's integrity and wonderfully enthusiastic, infectious personality that has propelled him to success. That's what made this book an enjoyable read too.'
— **Nigel Botterill**, Entrepreneur, marketer, author, speaker and business mentor

'Written in the first person, this is a compelling read and a vibrant account of a most extraordinary journey in a notoriously complex and challenging translation industry.

Unapologetic for exhibiting his own successful experience and unafraid that others can copy the same route he's taken "to become a successful business owner in a foreign country", David takes a reflective, witty and occasionally irreverent look at the professional world of localisation. Always generous in its advice, what makes this story so captivating is David's positive approach to life and business, his message of optimism and hope, and his profound belief that hard work, high standards and perseverance will always keep you afloat.

Certainly one of the most inspirational rags-to-riches entrepreneurs in the localisation field I've ever met!'

— **Prof Jorge Díaz-Cintas**, Centre for Translation Studies (CenTraS), University College London

'David's telling of his own story is on the one hand an entertaining and touching tale of triumph over adversity, how the power of self-belief can bring great achievements, and what can happen when one is driven to unlock one's own potential. On the other hand, beneath the affable and personable exterior of the author and main protagonist beats the relentless entrepreneurial heart of a highly astute, sharp and award-winning business owner.

Do not settle for being charmed by David's autobiographical openness; seek out and know that there are real commercial insights to be gained from David and his story, chief among them what it means and what is possible when you have *cojones* in business. Realise also that this book embodies the strategic and creative thinking, transparency and personal connection needed to excel in the modern entrepreneurial space, especially in a field as critical as the intersection of digital, multicultural and audiovisual media.

If you don't already know David, you will. If you haven't already been inspired by his story, you will. If your business is not yet working with him, for him or because of him, read the book. It's only a matter of time.'

— **Stewart Dickison**, Former manager and director at Technicolor

'As a fellow entrepreneur who's embarked on a not too dissimilar story (having moved to the UK in my early twenties and working in the language industry) I knew, after meeting David on several occasions (and being infused by his integrity, professionalism and energy), that this book would be full of life and great tips. It delivered, just as I had expected!

I would strongly advise anyone who is either thinking of starting in business or has done so already to grab this book with both hands, and soak up its well-presented and powerful messages.'

— **Nathalie Danon**, Director at Vici Language Academy

'In his book, David perfectly captures his journey from youngster to entrepreneur, sharing his insights and challenges along the way. This book proves that anything is possible and that obstacles can be overcome with the right attitude, actions and support.'

— **Adele Bryant**, Managing director at Process Clarity

SECOND EDITION

CHANCING YOUR ARM

HOW I MADE IT BIG IN BRITAIN

DAVID GARCÍA GONZÁLEZ

Rethink

First published in Great Britain in 2016 by Rethink Press (www.rethinkpress.com)

Second edition published 2023

© Copyright David García González

All rights reserved. No part of this publication may be reproduced, stored in or introduced into a retrieval system, or transmitted, in any form, or by any means (electronic, mechanical, photocopying, recording or otherwise) without the prior written permission of the publisher.

The right of David García González to be identified as the author of this work has been asserted by him in accordance with the Copyright, Designs and Patents Act 1988.

This book is sold subject to the condition that it shall not, by way of trade or otherwise, be lent, resold, hired out, or otherwise circulated without the publisher's prior consent in any form of binding or cover other than that in which it is published and without a similar condition including this condition being imposed on the subsequent purchaser.

Cover image © Shutterstock | AVA Bitter | In-Finity | Flas100

I want to dedicate this book to all entrepreneurs, business owners and people who are their own boss or are about to embark on this journey.

I know from my own experiences how difficult it can be, but also how rewarding this job/lifestyle is.

This book is a tribute to your struggles and successes and drives progress in an ever-changing and demanding world of business and technical innovation.

I salute you for your courage and determination.

The last few years have seen unprecedented challenges for business owners. If you have survived, never mind thrived, in these circumstances, I doubly salute you. It's been a ride, hasn't it?

Contents

Foreword	1
Introduction	5
PART ONE The Rain in Spain and Other Lessons in Linguistics	15
1 From Early Learning To Radio Gaga	17
2 A Flair For Linguistics	29
3 Educate, Speculate And Translate	39
PART TWO They Don't Even Speak English in England	53
4 Fortune At The End Of A Rainbow	55

5	The Hard Road And The Freeloader	71
6	Long Days, More Learning And GoLocalise	83

PART THREE Lend Me Your Ears for a While — 95

7	Friends, Colleagues, Covid And Change	97
8	Translation That Others Could Understand	121
9	A New World Of Ideas And Opportunity	131

PART FOUR The Big Lesson and the Way Forward — 143

10	Making Friends Makes Good Business Sense	145
11	Getting Older And Wiser And Running A More Mature Business	155

Conclusion	181
Acknowledgements	191
The Author	195

Foreword

One of my favourite ever comedy moments is the Four Candles sketch from the BBC comedy *The Two Ronnies*, written by the genius Ronnie Barker. The sketch opens with a throwaway joke as the hardware shopkeeper (Ronnie Corbett) hands a lady a roll of toilet paper, saying 'Mind how you go.' The lady exits and the shopkeeper is then confronted by a customer (Ronnie Barker), who is holding a shopping list. The customer requests what sounds like 'four candles'. The shopkeeper then takes out four candles, but the customer repeats his request, which confuses the shopkeeper. The customer rephrases his request to reveal he in fact wanted 'fork 'andles' (handles for garden forks). The dialogue continues with the customer asking for 'O's' (not hose or hoes, but a letter 'O' for the garden gate), 'peas' (not the letter 'P', a tin of peas), and 'pumps' (brown, size 9 – not a foot pump).

The scene ends with the shopkeeper taking offence at something written on the list, which is revealed to be 'billhooks'. The audience is intended to infer that the shopkeeper misread it as... well I'm sure you can imagine.

I was lucky enough to see the original sketch when it was first aired in the 1970s. The sound of belly laughter filled our living room but I recall, even as a ten-year-old, getting more and more tense and increasingly agitated and frustrated as the scene went on with the misinterpretation of the spoken words coming out of the TV.

Nearly 50 years on from *The Two Ronnies*, whilst the world around us has dramatically changed in terms of technological advancements, language barriers and translation needs are more important than ever. And this, thankfully, is where David comes in...

I've been fortunate to work closely with David as his scalability coach and business mentor for many years, originally within the Entrepreneurs Circle, where he has deservedly won a multitude of awards – not just for his business excellence and entrepreneurship, but for being the most inspiring member in 2015, which is quite an accolade with over 2,000 high-energy, driven business owners all competing for the same title.

FOREWORD

I was curious as to what to expect when David shared with me the intriguing title of his new book that he was busy penning (I hear *a lot* of clients and colleagues telling me they're writing their book but they inevitably get stuck midway through the draft. I always knew David would finish his – and bang on schedule – because he has that rare ability to be both visionary and an implementer, as you'll see from his engaging stories contained within each chapter). I know his business GoLocalise well, but I wasn't entirely sure how his personal story was going to translate into a business book.

When David gave me a draft to review, I bit his arm off and got stuck right in. I'd just published my own book, *I Don't Work Fridays*,[1] so to be on the other end was exciting – seeing the title, the book cover design and then the draft.

I *thought* I knew David well. I was immediately captivated by his personal story of growing up in a small Spanish town, hit by family tragedy at such an early age and then the challenges he faced not only as a lonely Spaniard settling in the UK, but in business and into the realms of entrepreneurialism. I now fully appreciate David's achievements and have a clear understanding as to why he is so driven and passionate about everything he puts his mind and heart to.

---

1 Norbury, M, *I Don't Work Fridays: Proven strategies to scale your business and not be a slave to it* (Rethink Press, 2016)

If there are two (well, three) things that I will personally take away from *Chancing Your Arm*, they are:

1. Learning lessons is *so* important and David shares these in abundance, whether they are personal or in business.
2. Entrepreneurship can be a lonely path to walk, but it doesn't have to be – you do not have to walk it alone.
3. Learning where phrases and words derive is fascinating. I am storing up all the wonderful lessons in language and the educational snippets so that I can beat my brother-in-law in this year's Christmas quiz.

In his closing chapters, David explains what an entrepreneur actually is. I won't reveal any spoilers, but I will say this: by knowing him, working with him and now reading this personal book, I have no doubt that David embodies the true spirit of an entrepreneur. You'd do well to read, enjoy and digest this book from the comfort of your armchair to learn the many lessons David has had to learn the hard way.

Martin Norbury, The Scalability Coach, Business Mentor of the Year 2015, and Author of #1 Amazon Bestseller *I Don't Work Fridays*

Introduction

The first edition of *Chancing Your Arm: How I made it big in Britain* certainly seemed to serve its purpose. I wanted the book to connect with people, help them get to know me and provide guidance, inspiration and even a little fun. It was never meant to sell millions, just prove a useful way to open doors, share my story and build trust in life and business. It has been revised in this second edition because my life and attitude towards my business have both changed since I first put pen to paper. The world of work, due to the Covid-19 global pandemic, also seems a different place than it was back then.

But more of that later.

Now, we must start at the beginning.

My name is David García González. I have developed a theory of life and business I call being 'bulletproof'. It means fearlessly thriving even in the face of adversity – without needing to wear a vest. You will see that this is a recurring theme which has become a central idea in my life, my business and everything I do. Life throws things at you sometimes, and when it does, you only have three choices: you can keep your head down, run away or stand and fight. If you are going to stand and fight (which is the only way to win), then you are going to need some good protection. For me, that protection includes:

- Being the best you can possibly be, as consistently as possible
- Learning from those around you who have already proved that what you are trying to achieve can work
- Listening attentively and applying the things that you learn
- Having respect for, interest in and a desire to help other people (especially those who deserve it)
- Being able to laugh about it all, even when things go wrong

My theory and the book you hold in your hands reflect the route I took to become a successful business owner in a foreign country and, ultimately, reach a welcome level of contentment in my personal life. It talks about me a lot, and I don't apologise for that.

INTRODUCTION

This is unashamedly my story. It is all about what I have learned to be true across stages in my life – from childhood in Spain and starting a business in London through to surviving a global pandemic, securing the future of my business and setting up a new home in the sunshine of Florida. Its real value, however, lies in interpreting how others have influenced me and providing lessons you can apply to your own stories. I hope it will provide an inspirational spark whether you're just starting on your journey or, like me, you have been through the early days and are facing new challenges.

The book is divided into four parts which are designed to be read sequentially. The narrative centres around stories that cover elements of my experiences to date – how I grew up in a northern Spanish town, discovered a love for linguistics and moved to the UK to study and work. They go on to tell how I found myself setting up my own business and then understanding the secret to maturing that business and realising its value. There are also relevant anecdotes about my personal life as I've grown older and wiser. Don't panic though, they are far from boring.

Interwoven throughout the text are 'breakouts' in the following two forms: Lessons, and Words.

Lessons: At various times I will break from the narrative to share a relevant business lesson. These are proven insights that I have discovered or been taught along the way, and are the real key to the book, containing ideas and truths which have helped shape my own success. Ultimately, these lessons point towards the bigger idea: the route to becoming bulletproof and being able to deal with whatever life throws in your path.

Words: My life revolves around words, whether they are verbal, written, translated, visually represented or implied. I am fascinated by the romance, potential and influence of language, so I have collected together some of my favourite linguistic mishaps, quirks and curiosities. These sections are for your enjoyment and entertainment, and might even win you a few trivia board games at Christmastime. It is lucky I love words because they're how I've chosen to earn a living. Translation is the business of propelling language around the globe and from culture to culture and, as I've delivered it over the years, I've picked up one or two anecdotes that add a bit of colour to my story – the Translation Interludes. They may prove useful too. If you are ever called 'an owl' in Hindi, for example, you'll thank me!

You will see a handful of words and phrases highlighted in **bold** throughout the text. These are key elements that have become important foundation stones for me, and I will come back to some of them at the end as a summary and aide-memoire.

In many ways, this was intended to be a book for people who want to make a career for themselves within the wonderful world of translation, localisation and linguistics. The more I thought about the content

I wanted to include, though, the more I realised how much more it had to offer. What I have learned could be valuable within any type of business, or for life in general. I have now looked back and applied the wisdom of age. I've done all this in a way that aids understanding of the challenges we all face in business. Please feel free to pay this understanding forward and share my ideas with others.

The idea of being bulletproof is central to the story for three reasons. Firstly, because you need to be able to stand up to the problems that you will unquestionably face in life. Secondly, you will get on better in work and life if you deliver a bulletproof performance. That doesn't mean you have to be perfect all of the time; it means being the best that you can be, every time. Thirdly, because being bulletproof will lead to happiness in the long run. This last point, I know, can be hard to believe when you're sweating blood establishing your small business in the first place. Trust me, though, it is true and a fact worth keeping in the back of your mind as you battle on.

You might think that bulletproof living and working sounds like a high standard to set, and maybe even a little unforgiving, but I am talking about an ordinary person becoming a high achiever. Everyone has the potential to do amazing things and I'm promoting the idea that you cannot remain at a 'standard' level and achieve 'above standard' results – that would be unfair to those who do work hard and apply the extra level of effort and commitment it takes to be excellent.

Some people do not have the opportunities that those living in the UK do. Even in this country, there can be wide gaps between the circumstances that people are born into, but everyone can take the cards they have been dealt and make the most of them. Whatever you choose to do, or are able to do, you can try harder than the person next to you and do better than them. That puts you ahead of the crowd and means that when the volley of bullets does come your way, you will have a much greater chance of surviving to fight another day.

The regular references to the idea of 'being bulletproof' reflect my perception of what this means to me personally and when I am looking to employ people in my business. Before I take you back to the 1980s and a small town in Spain, I'd like to emphasise some of the other things to look out for:

- **A process.** Becoming bulletproof does not happen overnight. It is a process which starts when you recognise your own human frailties and weaknesses. You grow a thick skin and develop a strong attitude by using the experiences life offers you and listening to its lessons. Everyone lives a different journey, but the same lessons are there for all of us to learn. It is up to each person to recognise, take hold of and apply these learnings.
- **A choice.** When you are young, your sole purpose in life is to have fun. It is difficult, perhaps impossible, for a fun-driven child to

comprehend that one day they will grow up and have to take responsibility for themselves, and some adults still continue to wrestle with this concept. When that fateful day of realisation dawns in your life, and in the days and months that follow, it is up to you which direction you choose to pursue. (The good news is that growing up well makes you better placed to enjoy fun for the rest of your life.)

- **A challenge.** The world is full of the 'ordinary', and it is no coincidence that the majority of things in life are, by default, those we refer to as 'average'. That is a fact of simple statistics, so it follows that to be better than average, you simply have to do more, and do it better than most other people. Whether it is to think smarter, practise harder, fight for longer, investigate deeper or become more resilient, you must outperform 'ordinary'.

- **A vision.** Having become a high achiever (and if you've chosen to rise to the challenge, you will), you must take your strengths and apply them correctly. If you have become bulletproof, or are on your way to getting there, then you've got to have a goal to direct your efforts towards. There is no point in being above average and staying in the same league as everyone else. Barcelona might win every match in the Segunda División, but without promotion where would their competition come from and how would they improve? They get better each week by playing their big-name rivals in La Liga.

CHANCING YOUR ARM

Before I start my story, let me introduce you to an idiom that sums up the value of taking measured risks in life: 'chancing your arm'. Being reckless is futile but, as medieval earl Gearóid FitzGerald demonstrates in this little tale, when you learn to read a situation, what seems like a big risk is well worth taking for the reward of victory.

> **WORDS: Chancing your arm**
>
> In the fifteenth century, there were two Anglo-Irish families, the Butlers and the FitzGeralds, who were constantly fighting each other for territory and the right to rule. In 1477 Gearóid FitzGerald became Lord Deputy at Dublin Castle, making him one of the most influential men in the land. This stirred up even more angst and rivalry between these warring factions, and

INTRODUCTION

> it all came to a head in a pitched battle in 1492, just outside of Dublin. Some senior members of the Butler family took refuge in the chapter house of St Patrick's Cathedral, claiming sanctuary and calling for a ceasefire. Gearóid stood outside and promised that if they came out, he would grant them safety and free passage in return for their surrender. The feud was so great that they didn't believe his words, so in a last-ditch effort to show good faith and end the fighting, Gearóid demonstrated an act of extreme courage.
>
> He took an axe and smashed a hole through the door, just wide enough for his arm. He then stuck his whole arm through so he and the Butlers could shake hands on the deal. This, of course, gave the Butlers an easy opportunity to chop old Gearóid's arm off, should they have wanted to. They didn't. Gearóid's faith was rewarded and the expression 'chancing your arm' became part of the English language.

My story is about how a naïve, easily distracted and largely unsuspecting Spaniard moved to live in a foreign country and learned to communicate with the locals. It details the pitfalls, the opportunities, the fun and the fears I faced. If you want to live, work and be successful within the context of the clash of cultures and idiosyncrasies posed by a foreign land, or if you find getting your message across difficult, even in your own language, then this book will help you. I hope, even though you may laugh with me as I share my story, that you'll take something valuable from my experiences. Most of all, I hope you'll come to understand that it is possible to use your differences for the common good.

Coming to England as a foreigner and setting up a business was not an easy challenge for me. In fact, it was a massive risk; but, as you will see as you read through this book, it was one influenced by ongoing learning and becoming aware of the different types of people I'd meet on the journey. Being able to take the appropriate risks when the right moment arrives hasn't stopped as I have aged. The process is an ongoing one. The lessons never stop.

Now you have a little insight into my story and the world of localisation. I hope you enjoy the journey and, more importantly, discover some things to help you become more bulletproof.

PART ONE
THE RAIN IN SPAIN AND OTHER LESSONS IN LINGUISTICS

1
From Early Learning To Radio Gaga

I think my initial interest in languages came as a result of being packed off by my grandparents to attend extra lessons to keep me busy. As I was born to young parents (my mum was nineteen when I arrived) in Gijón, a small town in the north of Spain, it was inevitable that my extended family would be heavily involved in my upbringing. This meant that my grandma and grandpa's traditional values and beliefs were imposed on me (with love), and I spent many an evening attending after-school English and Italian lessons. Of course, they weren't even Grandma and Grandpa in those early days; I knew them as Ito and Ita (shortened from the Spanish words for grandparents – *abuelito* and *abuelita*), and even though back then those quaint and cosy titles were a result of my underdeveloped pronunciation skills, that is how I still refer to them to this day.

The mantra of Ito and Ita's generation was, 'The best thing that you can do for your children is give them an education', and so that was how I was brought up. In truth, the extra lessons in language were no hardship at all – I was fascinated by the romantic potential and unlimited possibility of foreign words.

My dad passed away when I was a teenager, and my mum came to rely more and more on the rest of the family to help look after my brother and me. They did the job well, and there were always lots of things going on, including great encouragement (which they loosely interpreted as 'insistence') for us to get involved in activities: sports, schooling, music and so on. From an early age, however, long before the loss of my dad and the overflow of education, I loved my mum most of all. If anyone came between me and her, I would just bite them.

No, that is not a mistake – I really did bite them.

The first time this happened was on my first day at nursery, just a few minutes after being dropped off. It is not uncommon for a child to have a screaming, shouting tantrum on that most traumatic of occasions when the thought crosses their mind, *Why is my mum leaving me here?* For me, the initial reaction quickly grew into, *I will never see her again – she clearly doesn't love me anymore.* From that mere seedling of an idea, sheer panic rapidly evolved, and before long the sense of rejection became what felt like a veritable forest of despair. I do not have a clear memory of this event, which may be why I am so unashamedly sharing it with you, but apparently that was the exact moment I sank my gnashers into the teacher's arm.

Having acquired a taste for vengeance at what appeared to my eyes to be a heartless act of parental treachery, I wasn't finished. I feigned a degree of calmness for a while before going on to bite three of the other children – innocent kids who had, up until that point, been handling their first-day experience rather better than I was. It wasn't until I was given my chorizo sandwiches at lunchtime that I truly calmed down. There are certain treats in life that always seem to be able to take my mind away from the trauma of the moment, and that wouldn't be the last time chorizo would do the trick for me.

In the absence of a familiar face, confused by the sudden loss of security and unable to communicate my anxiety in any other way at the time, I misread the situation and misused my mouth. Thinking about it, I assume my mum must have explained to me what was going to happen prior to her walking away that morning, but for whatever reason the message didn't sink in (not as far as my teeth would, at any rate). Her language didn't compute, so I didn't co-operate, and we can all be guilty of this from time to time, can't we? OK, maybe not the biting, but certainly misunderstanding what is meant by someone else's words and actions, especially under stressed or unfamiliar circumstances.

> **LESSON: Good communication in the first instance saves a lot of pain in the end**
>
> One of the most common results of a breakdown in communication is that one party will get increasingly frustrated with the other, or possibly both with each other. Unchecked or ignored, this could lead to a breakdown in the entire relationship, or at least put it under unnecessary pressure. Any further attempts at communication can then become strained and open the door for even wider misunderstandings.
>
> It might help if you were bulletproof. Effective communication between different languages is not simply about translating or relaying the words in a correct format; rather, it is the art of making sure that the listener understands your message. This means knowing the audience well, including all their preconceptions, wants, concerns and prejudices.
>
> Effective translation can help to keep misunderstanding off the menu.

The biting incident was not Mum's fault – how was she to know that I would react that way? In fact, I was developing into quite a naughty child in general, always on the search for the quickest way into and out of trouble. Getting away with it became quite an art form for me – much to the annoyance of my brother, who often took the blame for my mischief. While my tendency to bite those who upset me faded away after a few years, I've continued developing my propensity for naughtiness ever since, so watch out…

As I got older and made my way through school, my love for languages grew just as much as my distrust of anything mathematical. My approach was far too haphazard for numbers and science, and at that age, attention to detail seemed too much like hard work – I think it was the idea that a slight error at the beginning of a calculation could knock out the entire sequence of numbers and ruin the final result that bothered me.

Linguistics, however, came naturally to me. I loved the passion, flow and vivacity of the words and the flexibility of the final product. The fact that there were so many ways to convey the same message captured my attention and fuelled my imagination, and learning new languages opened up the door to even more possibilities.

> **LESSON: Bad translation just doesn't add up**
>
> Ironically, my entire business philosophy today hangs on the very element of science which caused me to hate it with such a passion in my youth. Over my many years learning the ropes of my profession, and as a business owner in a foreign country, I have come to recognise that the key to effective translation is accuracy. In other words, the finest of details really do matter. I would even go as far as to say that, in the translation and localisation industries at least, right first time = happy customers.

> **WORDS: Translation interlude**
>
> The phrase 'learning the ropes' is an extension of the nautical term 'knowing the ropes', which describes when a sailor can tie the full and abundant range of knots needed to sail safely and efficiently. It takes skill, commitment and experience for a novice to get to this point, and often lives can depend upon a sailor's expert knot-tying – particularly under pressure. In Spanish, however, you simply wouldn't use this phrase (although we are equally proud of our seafaring heritage). Instead, you would say, *'Cogerle el tranquillo'*. This translates literally as 'to get the knack of', which means the same thing, but without the need for a seafaring explanation to those who don't have English as a first language.
>
> In translation, details like this can have a massive effect on how easily a message gets across, because properly understanding the intention of the text is paramount to avoiding the wrong transfer of meaning. Otherwise, you could end up with a beautifully written story conveying ideas or concepts that have no bearing on the writer's

> original intention, and that constitutes an enormous no-no in translation.
>
> Keep on reading and you'll soon get the *tranquillo*.

Like most teenagers, I had no idea what I wanted to do at the age of fourteen, but it seemed I was always drawn towards things that involved flair, fun and interaction with people. It was at that age that I first managed to get my voice on the airwaves. Together with a couple of my school friends, I started broadcasting a radio show every Wednesday evening from a local radio station called Onda Verde, which translates as Green Wave (or, more literally, Wave Green). The three of us filled a full hour and a half with music, conversation and interviews – basically having a bit of a laugh. My mum still has all of the tapes – she loves me a lot too.

It was probably this experience that sparked my interest in journalism and production, and it was my first entrepreneurial exploit. Before long I discovered that I had a burning desire to get my voice heard by the masses. My auntie and uncle knew a DJ at Radio Vetusta, a larger radio station about fifteen miles away in Oviedo, and so I asked if I could have a bit of airtime. This resulted in a sidekick role on a national show, which meant that I spent Friday evenings talking to the nation while also chattering away to the handful of people who bothered to tune in to Onda Verde on a Wednesday.

The Friday evening show was all about pets, and my job was to research each week's animal. It was pretty deep stuff: 'Hello, everyone – this week we are talking about rabbits. Does anyone have a rabbit?' We would take a few calls, and then I would relay some of the knowledge that I had gleaned from books and talking to experts: 'Did you know that there are over fifty breeds of rabbit recognised by the British Rabbit Council? Lizards are more popular than rabbits as pets. It is easy to train rabbits to use litter boxes…'

The show's host would fill in with a few more questions and then say something like 'What do you think, David?', trying to keep it as interesting as possible. I couldn't help wondering if a more stimulating subject matter might have created more of a buzz, but it was, at the least, a good introduction to proper journalism and radio broadcasting.

In comparison, my Wednesday night show was a lot more out there. My two friends, Maria and Eduardo, were similarly attracted to mischief, although probably not quite as much as I was; we were fourteen and it was only a small-scale amateur station, but we were keen to do our job well, and even managed to get celebrities of a sort on the show. We aimed for people our listeners didn't like much and put them on the spot, recording the interviews then playing them with some edits. It wasn't beyond our teenage minds to mix the questions and answers around a little before broadcasting the final edit, adding in a few sound effects to create what we saw as pure on-air hilarity – mostly aimed at impressing our school friends. This was how I came to know that nothing creates better ratings than a little controversy. Hey – I was embarking on a career in journalism, learning to give scope to the truth.

Because we were an official, albeit amateur, station, we would get invites to events and concerts and were allowed to go into the press room. This meant we came into contact with people whom we could persuade to come on the show, including Grammy-winning Spanish bands of the time like La Oreja de Van Gogh, which translates as Van Gogh's Ear.

Having gone on to set up my own business, it is only now, looking back on those days, that I realise this was my first customer-accumulation experience. In a sense, you could say that we built the show on word-of-mouth marketing. When we started, no one was listening, so we went around the school telling all of our friends to tune in, asking them to get their parents to listen too. Then we asked my aunt and uncle (who owned a local restaurant) for a free meal voucher to give away as a prize, which got the lines ringing for our phone-ins, and before we knew it, we had created a local radio phenomenon. We knew we had hit the big time when we first gave away a free dinner to someone we didn't know – fame at last.

> **LESSON: Lessons learned from a small-town radio show**
>
> Marketing is a broad term for most small businesses, covering any activities that try and increase sales. Obviously things have changed a lot in recent decades with the emergence of the Internet, but the principles

remain the same. I didn't know it at the time, but my Onda Verde adventure was a genuine exercise in how to create, engage with and grow an enthusiastic following. This is why Twitter, Facebook and other social media channels are the most popular news media today – they work.

Let me explain the process in its simplest form. This is a two-step marketing model that translates across almost any business, anywhere in the world.

Step 1 – Know your audience. It is true that my teenage friends and I just wanted to have fun on the radio, but we also had a burning desire for people to listen to us. It wasn't enough just to be heard; we wanted our peers to tune in and think that we were funny. We wanted a taste of fame. Whenever we got together for a kind of board meeting to discuss the content for the next show, we were always driven by one question – what would impress our audience?

Has your marketing (or indeed your product or service) been designed to answer that question?

Step 2 – Engage your audience. Each Thursday morning (the day after our show) we would be the centre of attention at school for a while (which we loved), but we still had questions for our school friends. We wanted to know what had made them laugh the most, what they had enjoyed and what else they would like to hear. In return for entertaining them, we asked (in reality, it was probably more along the lines of told) them to get other people to listen: friends, family and other kids at school.

Do you encourage your customers to talk positively about you? After all, there is no better advert than

> independent voices saying how much they love you. The result is a self-perpetuating marketing machine, applicable online and offline, which, properly executed, will eventually do all the work for you.

This was how I first learned that becoming great at communication is a powerful way to get on in the world, and that it is a lot of fun too. In Chapter 2, I move from out-and-out fun into education. Still fun, but not quite as raucous.

2
A Flair For Linguistics

In my town, school officially finished at 2 o'clock in the afternoon (we started early), but because of my extra-curricular education regime, I then attended a specialist academy for languages that was an optional extra for kids in the area. One of my teachers, an Irish lady called Jenny, made the learning exciting and fun, and had a real impact on my language education. She was the one who first introduced me to *Muzzy* and *Mr Bean*, and I will always be grateful to her for fanning my passion for language in this way.

If you have not heard of *Muzzy in Gondoland*, it is an animated BBC film that was developed specifically to help children learn English as a second language. It tells the story, highlighting numbers, colours, times, objects and other everyday things, of how Muzzy (an alien) rescues his true love in the royal palace of Gondoland. As an educational tool, it has been so successful that it has since been dubbed for use in a multitude of languages, from Russian to Romanian and even Mandarin. Once again, the power of engaging with a target audience at the right level has had a massive impact on the target audience! This is so important when it comes to translation because, just as with marketing, you need to know who your audience is before you start.

At the other end of the scale, Jenny became my hero when she sat my fellow students and me down in front of the TV (a treat in itself) and pressed the 'play' button to introduce us to the comic genius of *Mr Bean* in full colour. What a revelation that was. For the first time in my life, I understood how humour, emotion and sheer shameless delight could be transmitted from one human being to another without a single word being uttered. Unlike *Muzzy*, which was all about learning the English words for different objects and actions, *Mr Bean* was a masterclass in true communication.

> **LESSON: Comic genius or communications expert?**
>
> Slapstick and visual-only content (when it is done well) transcends language, culture and understanding. This is a point well worth remembering when you're involved in any kind of translation project or communicating your business message. Did you know that the *Mr Bean* TV series has been shown in 190 countries around the

> world, without translation, dubbing or subtitles? There have been few productions that would be able to match this, and for that reason alone, *Mr Bean* represents a lot of important wisdom in the world of communication and translation – even if he is a total schmuck.

I left the school education system at seventeen with an armful of qualifications, and passed my PAU exam, the standard in Spain to enable you to go to university, but I still didn't know exactly what I wanted to do. Then, as I wandered along a path towards more study at university, chance and happenstance intervened and sent me searching out the hustle and bustle of the UK.

My great aunt and uncle ran a little café in Chalton Street, just off Euston Road in London, and invited my best friend, David, and me to stay with them. For four weeks, straight out of school, we soaked up the culture and character of life in London. I was instantly hooked, and the fact that my great aunt and uncle served my favourite chorizo sandwiches in the café helped with any lingering homesickness.

My family was still keen for me to take the further education route, so I applied to and got accepted at Essex University, and started the following year. Jenny helped there too, persuading me that living and studying in Colchester would be a good move for my education and future. It was also a chance to spread my wings, leave behind the Spanish small-town mindset and see a bit more of the world.

> **WORDS: Translation interlude**
>
> To the best of my knowledge, 'spread your wings' is one of those phrases which actually does translate into most languages. This is likely due to the literality of the picture that it paints: raising yourself up above the status quo to reach new heights and discover new worlds beyond the reach of your existing circumstances.

I studied a combined degree in linguistics, languages and computers at Essex University while living on the campus in my first year. That meant I met lots of new people, made friends and got to know the culture and language a whole lot better.

> **LESSON: Never underestimate the power of knowing your customers well**
>
> It goes without saying that living and studying in a country is the best way to learn its language. In the same manner, the best way to understand a potential client, or any person that you are trying to impress, is to get closer to the real them. When you want to communicate a message clearly, the listener is the most important factor in the entire transaction. If you understand them fully, almost as if you have walked in their shoes and shared a part of their life, then you will be in a position of strength when creating the message.

After three years, I left university in June 2002 with a BA Honours in teaching English as a foreign language

(TEFL) and computer applications, and a minor in Italian. I have wracked my brains trying to remember some of the things that happened while I was there which might be valuable life lessons. I've sat down with countless bottles of red wine and spent several wild nights out on the town trying to pull out some wisdom to share with you from those wild times. I've slept in late and wasted hours laughing with friends and enjoying myself in a vain effort to recall just one speck of advice to aid you in your quest for business success, but none of this has helped in any way, shape or form. My efforts to remember the three years I spent at Essex University have done nothing but recreate blurred half-memories, a few hangovers and some secret smiles.

The one useful thing that did come to mind, though, was that I read a lot, and whenever I picked up a book or an article about linguistics, one name came up time after time. Jorge Díaz-Cintas is one of the world's authorities on translation, the director of the Centre for Translation Studies at University College London (UCL), and a true expert. He was also one of the first bulletproof people I ever learned about within translation, and many years later I met him and we became friends. It's funny how life has a way of doing things like that to you.

After university, the whole 'What do I do next?' question came up again. My fellow students were going off to do a whole range of different things: years out, more study, graduate positions and the like, but I was still totally undecided. One of my friends had become a corporate lawyer a year earlier and even as a junior he was making

£50k a year, so I decided I would like a piece of that for myself. On this occasion it was the lure of a healthy income that helped me make up my mind, but it turned out to be a bad decision in the end – probably because it was driven by the wrong motivation. I clearly hadn't achieved the right qualification to become a lawyer, but I didn't want to waste my language skills, so I took a master's in applied translation studies (specialising in legal translation) at the London Metropolitan University.

To cut a long, boring, totally regrettable story short, I passed but hated the subject. (I would like to point out at this juncture that I loved my tutor – it was just the work itself which sapped my joy.) Writing the dissertation for that particular course was one of the most tedious and soul-destroying experiences of my life. It was around 10,000 words long, entitled 'Spanish Legal Translation: Translation between languages and different legal systems' and was mostly made up of footnotes. Although I got quite a good grade for the course, the work itself would have had a good shot at winning a prize for the most boring dissertation ever written. **Never again**.

> LESSON: Knowing your why is far more important than discovering the how
>
> It was only in later years, after reading a book called *Start with Why* by Simon Sinek,[2] that I realised why I had hated legal translation so much as a subject.

---

[2] Sinek, S, *Start with Why: How great leaders inspire everyone to take action* (Penguin, 2011)

My motivation had been all wrong. You see, I had been attracted to an element of the legal profession which fitted my skill set purely because I perceived that there was money to be made. Don't get me wrong, I have no objection to financial gain, and I certainly don't view profit, ambition or wealth as dirty words. In fact, I would strongly recommend anyone who is considering starting a business, freelancing or studying for a new career to ask themselves: 'Will I be able to make enough money doing this?' You would be abundantly daft not to take this into consideration – **you need money to live**.

Please understand me here. Although I do not believe that money is the principle consideration, if you disregard it altogether you will fall into difficulties eventually. There is, however, a way to enjoy your life today rather than simply making money for the future, and it involves finding your why. Work out what your passion is, then you can search out ways to turn that passion into a viable, robust and scalable business to give you both a present and a future.

If there is one big lesson I hope you learn from reading this book, then it is this: first and foremost, work at something that you love. If you do that sincerely and intelligently, the rewards will always follow.

WORDS: Translation interlude

Before I go on with my story and detail my eventual path to entrepreneurship, let's have a look at the importance of knowing what you want to say and how to say it effectively.

One of the things I realised as I learned more about English and the many nations that speak it as a first language, is that it is global; but it is not as ubiquitous as you might think, with at least 75% of the world's population speaking no English at all. This means that accurate translation is, and will continue to be for the foreseeable future, fundamental for connecting with a global audience. (As you will see later in this book, it is vital to local communication too.)

The biggest problem with the task of clearly conveying messages across language barriers is that some words don't translate clearly – if at all.

For example, the Scottish have words that the English don't, one example of which describes that most awkward of moments when you are in the middle of introducing someone and forget their name. The word is *tartle*, and, while it may be a useful one to add to the more general English vocabulary, it would be far better to remember people's names in the first place.

> Then there is one of the most beautiful and romantic single words for a sentiment which most other languages (as far as I am aware) need a full sentence to express. In Arabic, the word *ya'aburnee* conveys someone's heartfelt desire to die before the one they love dies, so as to avoid the pain of living without them. This sentiment was best captured in English by the great poet Winnie the Pooh: 'If you live to be a hundred, I want to live to be a hundred minus one day, so I never have to live a day without you.'[3] The literal translation of the word *ya'aburnee* is 'you bury me', but that doesn't quite capture the romantic tragedy, love, loss and passion of its true meaning. I like Winnie's version too, although his surname in itself can cause a few translation problems around the world, I can tell you.
>
> Whether you are expressing an undying love or having a senior moment in the Highlands, understanding differences in language is useful. It is much more effective if you consider your listeners' ears and use words that they might actually understand.

In the next chapter, I'll share my post-education experiences and the lessons I learned as I entered the real world and took on my first (albeit short-lived) 'proper' job.

---

3   Milne, AA, *Not That It Matters* (Methuen, 1926)

3
Educate, Speculate And Translate

After learning a big lesson in my venture into full-time education, I decided it was time to leave that arena behind for good. It was time to earn.

After a short job search, I landed a paid position as a junior project manager for a technical translation company in London. This only lasted six months before I started working freelance while studying for another master's degree, but it was still my first true taste of an actual 'job'. Looking back, I think it was that experience which kick-started my craving for entrepreneurship and forging my own path in life. My passion was rapidly changing towards stronger flavours and a more exciting working environment, and the thought of co-ordinating the translation of a 10,000-word technical manual for a new telephone or piece of software in fifteen to twenty languages simply didn't inspire me.

My six-month stint working in a medium-sized yet lifeless organisation taught me another massive lesson: how not to motivate your staff. As a first foray into working life, it was not an enjoyable one, but, as is often the case when you face a bit of a trial, this unpleasant experience lit a passion to create better ones.

The feeling of working in that environment is still vivid, and now, all these years later, it helps me focus on loving my staff. You may identify with what I am about to describe, but if you don't then make sure you give your boss an extra big smile next time you see them, because if your workplace is not like this, then they deserve it.

There were about fifty staff working in a large open-plan office with the boss sitting in sectioned-off headquarters at the far end of the room. There was a clear glass wall between us, but it may as well have been made of steel for all the good its transparency did anyone. Although there were no rules pinned up on the wall, the ironically unspoken rule was that we were not allowed to speak during the working day, and the suggestion lingered in the air that typing too loud would be equally frowned upon. Most of the staff went for a walk at lunchtime out of a sheer thirst for conversation or an exchange of human emotion.

The atmosphere was foreboding enough to leave us in no doubt that a hierarchy existed in the place: it was stifling to the soul. The lack of flexibility and absence of friendliness were echoed in the heavy productivity expectation, and the work itself was terminally boring – we were tasked with the quality control and review of household equipment instruction documents.

If you are responsible for staff, in any shape or form, please don't make them work in a place like this. I think I would rather write a 10,000-word law dissertation each day than have to live through that again.

By the time my six-month sentence was over, my impression of white goods had almost robbed my life of colour, and I'd had enough of discovering my purpose. I needed some direction, and it was time to get serious and apply myself 'on purpose' instead.

The part-time course that I took alongside my first foray into freelancing (translation, subtitling and voice-over) was done online through Universidad Autónoma de Barcelona (UAB). It was more education (a comfort zone for me), but it was the first time I had chosen to study something with a specific reason behind it. I finally realised what it was that I wanted to do.

The degree focused on dubbing, subtitling, video game localisation and other audiovisual translation topics. I enjoyed translation not just as a job, but for the joy, vitality, life and passion of language. It was about opening up people's ability to communicate in real-life environments, face-to-face and personally, not just swapping one word for its twin in another tongue. I loved the language of communication, so I set my attention on doing just that. It took a while, but I could finally see that you have to **love it before you can earn from it**.

> ### LESSON: Don't settle for second best; keep looking until you find your number one
>
> It seems strange to me that a parent, teacher or family friend will ask a young child, often just four or five, a grown-up question: 'What do you want to be when you grow up?' Perhaps one in 100 kids will go on to become a firefighter, a doctor or an astronaut, but do we really expect someone so young to have the clarity required to answer that question? Surely the vast majority of people chop and change, dream and forget, before they finally stumble upon something of consequence that they might enjoy. Then again, I am convinced that (as sad as it may be) most people never reach a decent level of contentment in their working life. Regardless of the possibilities they were encouraged to create and dream about as children, they end up working in a nine-to-five dead-end job from which they never escape.
>
> If you are reading this at the start of your journey, then please pay close attention to the next few paragraphs. If you are some way into your working life and any of the last paragraph rang true, then **it is never too late to make a change**.

It was in 2002, when I was twenty-three years old, that I finally started to gain clarity on what might keep me excited about getting up in the mornings for the rest of my life. As you will know from my story so far, the whole linguistics thing was initially a coincidental circumstance of my upbringing – I never chose to study languages so intensively. Had my early life played out a little differently then perhaps I might never have travelled at all. I could have studied politics or dropped out of school to work on a building site. These routes could have been equally successful and drawn out another passion from within me, a far call from the path that I eventually took. Because of my upbringing, something about language connected with me, lit a spark and became like a beacon deep inside my heart.

That means for me, and probably for you too, there is not necessarily a single path you need to find before you can reach contentment. There will be lots of things out there in this big, wide world of ours that interest you, and all you need to do is keep looking until you find one. To be truly happy in life, what you choose to pursue has to be something that you are genuinely passionate about, or you will always feel you are missing something. I can't help you discover what that might be, but you will know it when you find it. Likewise, I can't promise you that going for it will be easy, but if it is something you believe in it will be worth it in the end.

It doesn't matter if you haven't identified what it is yet – no matter what age you are. There is always time to change or fine-tune your goals until you discover the treasure that you can set your sights towards. As long as you go in the right direction, are honest enough with yourself to change course and in tune enough with your heart, you will get there.

> That is what happened to me in 2002, and I'm certain it could be the same for everyone else because I hear the same story (different details) from the other business owners and entrepreneurs I mix with every day. Far too many people settle for second best simply because option one hasn't happened yet, or worse still because they never discover what option one looks like. I feel sorry for those people because, with a little more drive, their story could be beautifully translated into the language of success and contentment.
>
> It is an important step for any would-be entrepreneur to recognise the real goal for them. Find the something that you enjoy doing as well as it giving you commercial success. This might only happen in stages; it was certainly that way for me, but if you are listening to your heart *and* your head, it will always reveal itself in the end.

Starting off a new career as a freelancer from scratch can be a little daunting, and I went into it naïvely, but I was determined, and in the end my ignorance meant that I could overcome my fear and do what had to be done, regardless. Even if you get to the 'this is where my passion is leading me' discovery, you still need to find some customers. To deal with that problem, you need to bring two important questions into play. Firstly, does anyone actually want what you are so excited about doing? And secondly, who are they and where are you going to find enough of them to make your business profitable?

When I started freelancing I didn't worry too much about any of that – I just started spamming everyone.

> **WORDS: Translation interlude**
>
> 'Spamming' is the practice of sending unsolicited (and certainly unwanted) bulk email messages. To qualify as true spam, they must be sent frequently in large quantities, always to an indiscriminate set of recipients, and have commercial content. In simple terms, it is an annoying and, under some circumstances, illegal practice.
>
> Oddly, the act of spamming was named after a *Monty Python* sketch from the 1970s in which Spam (a cheap luncheon meat) is included in every meal option on a café menu. While the word (and certainly the practice) is common in most languages and societies around the world today, its origin is not as widely known, the problem being that to explain the origin to a speaker for whom English is not their first language, you'd need to start by explaining *Monty Python* to them. Good luck with that.

In my defence, not only was I unaware that I was spamming, but I also didn't know what else to do. I recognised that I had bills to pay and a dream to build, and I had to start finding customers somewhere.

Now, if there is one strong quality I have (which can be seen as either positive or negative), it is stubbornness. If you have even an ounce of this in you then, when it comes to your business at least, I would encourage you to cultivate it. If you could add a little persistence into the mix too, and stay focused on the dream that

I talked about earlier, then you could become a formidable force destined for success.

To start with, I joined lots of online forums and chat rooms for translators, set up a profile on loads of sites and got myself on the national directory for freelance translators. Then I became active and got noticed in the industry by being involved. Over time, I managed to create myself a database of hundreds of companies that I could work for, and I made sure they knew me. I wrote a CV and crafted a sales letter and email campaign. Then I sent these out and phoned everyone as often as I needed to until they listened to my offer. Some of them must have got sick of my emails (and my voice), but some gave me work.

All this brings me nicely back to my flirtation with spamming. This was long before I learned anything about automation (most spamming nowadays is done with the press of a button), so I individually created every piece I sent out. I found the name of the decision maker for each company and researched and wrote a little bit about the business so they felt they were the one I wanted to freelance for. It took a lot of time, and an enormous amount of commitment, effort and stubborn persistence to succeed (which will hopefully lessen any bad feeling you might have developed for me when I admitted to having been a spammer).

Just to be clear about spamming, it is only a dodgy practice if the emails are unsolicited. If you have built a database of fans and customers who want to hear from you, then you can mass-market until your bank account is bulging. The trick is turning your cold call (unexpected and unfriendly) into a warm call (welcomed and useful).

There were times during my early days as a freelancer when it would have been easier to give up. If nothing had happened, it is possible that I might have done, although I don't think that I would have stopped trying to find work. I would have just looked at other ways to get the same result. There are two reasons for this: firstly, my heart now knew exactly what it wanted, and secondly, it *really* wanted it.

The result of my activity was a few freelancing jobs from various companies, and because I knew how hard I had worked to get them, I made sure I did a great job each time. This meant that my name got around a bit, and my reputation as being reliable and professional followed the name. Without patting myself on the back too much, I was what I look for in a translator. I had started to present myself as what I think of today as being bulletproof.

As is usually the case with a diligent and determined approach to good practice, my efforts eventually coincided with good fortune. One fine day I received an approach from Technicolor to work as a project manager in their subtitling department. I'd finally arrived at the start of the rainbow.

With that happy thought, how about a few more entertaining and educational idioms to finish off the chapter?

> **WORDS: Translation interlude**
>
> Every language has its quirks, but for me English produces some of the most entertaining and, from a translator's point of view, baffling idioms of all. Consider what a 'couch potato' could possibly sound like to someone hearing the expression for the first time. Their thought process might go along the lines of a vegetable that you grow in your living room, or perhaps a potato big enough to be used as a chair. You would have to take quite a large leap of imagination to end up with a lazy slob who sits around watching TV all day, which makes you wonder whom the person who first coined the phrase was thinking of.
>
> Likewise, when Shakespeare decided that Mark Antony would open his famous speech (in the play *Julius Caesar*)

with the words, 'Friends, Romans, countrymen, lend me your ears',[4] little did he know the trouble it would cause translators for centuries afterwards. There is logic and poetry to the phrase, and far be it from me to question the Bard's influence on the language, but really? How gruesome a suggestion for the unprepared reader of a foreign language to try and understand.

Another one that is a bit random for speakers where English is not their native language is the idea of having 'butterflies in your stomach'. Hmmm, tasty. Is this clearly a description of a feeling? Why else would you have butterflies inside you? They are certainly not served in any restaurant that I know.

This is exactly why getting to grips with translation is so important. It is only to a native speaker, who has lived, breathed and soaked up a language (with its

---

4   Shakespeare, W, *Julius Caesar* (Penguin Classics, 2015)

oddities and idiosyncrasies) all of their life, that these phrases are clear. How can someone who is learning a language or trying to translate it be expected to know whether something is literal or metaphorical? It is not beyond the realms of imagination to believe that eating butterflies is a delicacy in some cultures. In fact, it might be reasonable to think that doing so gives the eater courage, so the exact opposite of the intended meaning could easily be assumed.

Logic and common sense do not always come into it. Imagine being shown something during a cookery show that is easy, perhaps the basics of applying icing as decoration, and the presenter says, 'It's a piece of cake.' What are you supposed to think?

Going back to having butterflies in your stomach, apparently this is a saying that was introduced fairly recently. The first reference to butterflies describing

> feelings of anxiety was recorded in 1908,[5] and it was not until the 1940s that the current use of the phrase became commonplace. We tend to think of idioms like these as relics of antiquity, with a romantic origin story waiting to be discovered, but in truth they are simply things that are relevant to the times. I particularly like the most modern variation on this idea, because it is an encouragement to overcome the anxiety.
>
> Let me explain. The thought is that nerves are natural, and the fact that we get nervous (the proverbial fluttery feeling in our stomach) means that we are alive. It is part of the way that we are made and a feature of our fight or flight survival mechanism, making us more alert and ready to react. The key is to be aware that fear and nerves are a chemical reaction rather than something real, and we can control them. (I won't get too sidetracked here as this is a book on life, business and language, not neurolinguistic programming.) With the thought of controlling their nerves in mind, someone (the phrase is generally attributed to former footballer Steve Bull) came up with a modern take on the same phrase: 'Nerves and butterflies are fine – they're a physical sign that you're mentally ready and eager. The trick is to get the butterflies to fly in formation.'

Part Two of my story is all about working and building a reputation as an expert in a particular market (for me it was localisation) in a foreign country. Talking of markets, one of the strangest things I heard about when I first arrived in England was a 'flea market'.

---

5   Tréguer, P, 'Butterflies in one's stomach: Meaning and origin', Word Histories (22 March 2021), https://wordhistories.net/2021/03/22/butterflies-stomach, accessed 30 March 2023

CHANCING YOUR ARM

Put yourself in the shoes of a foreigner and try to imagine the picture that might paint in your mind.

The market I had arrived in was on a much bigger and scarier scale. Many of the lessons I will share with you were learned in the UK, but will be relevant for any settler in any country in the world. In the next chapter I will describe how I overcame my nerves by working for a global giant, and eventually trained my butterflies to fly together in the right direction.

PART TWO
THEY DON'T EVEN SPEAK ENGLISH IN ENGLAND

4
Fortune At The End Of A Rainbow

In 2005 I started working with Technicolor, an experience which couldn't have been further removed from my first dark brush with an office environment. Its people were lively, the business ethic was vibrant and full of vision, and I fell head over heels in love with my industry at last. It was a great place to work and learn, and I was surrounded by people who were experts in their various roles.

Bearing a name that is synonymous with the birth of colour film in the early 1900s and responsible for many perennial Christmas favourites, Technicolor is part of the backbone of the film industry. Without its innovation, we would never have enjoyed *The Wizard of Oz*, *Singin' in the Rain*, *Snow White and the Seven Dwarfs* or *Fantasia*. Today, it remains one of the leading media and entertainment companies in the world, providing innovative audio and video technologies for the film industry, and it was where I cut my teeth in the commercial world of translation services.

> **WORDS: Idioms**
>
> To 'cut one's teeth' is a reference to babies' teeth cutting through their gums and becoming useful, suggesting that the babies are learning how to use these sharp new additions to their eating arsenal, often with a bit of pain. The idiom today describes how someone takes the basic skills they have learned and applies them in a real-life environment, and in doing so accelerates the acquisition of new skills while consolidating the proven wisdom of the basics. In essence, they're taking the lessons out of the classroom and making them practical, which can, of course, involve the pain of learning too.

This idiom might need a bit of explanation if it were being translated into another language, unless you were translating a piece on the early lives of vampires and werewolves. (I suspect that Technicolor might have done some work on the *Twilight* films in recent years.)

After a few years of freelancing, becoming part of this huge organisation was quite a step for me, but it was an invaluable one because it showed me how big companies work. I was a project manager, which meant that I pulled together all of the resources needed to complete a specific job for a client, and they were exciting projects: creating the subtitles, dubbing and translations for a whole range of TV series and blockbuster movies. Often these productions needed to be made available in twenty or thirty different languages, covering all of Europe, Asia and the rest of the world.

As you can imagine, it was quite a task to ensure that every translation reflected a perfect representation of the original dialogue. That was where I first learned to identify and rely on outsourced individual translators whom I deemed to be bulletproof. I speak three languages well and, as a result, I have a slight understanding of several associated languages, but that didn't help me to check the quality and accuracy of over thirty different translations of an entire movie (or a billion-dollar franchise). This was a serious business, and I simply could not do it on my own. In this industry, and I imagine it's similar everywhere, there is no better resource than a safe, reliable and consistent pair of hands (or a voice). I fell in love with bulletproof talent back then, and I'd still go a long way to secure its services today.

It is an unfortunate but true fact of marketing that a bad product well marketed will always outsell a good product, badly marketed. In most industries, that is enough for the smart marketers to do better than the best performers, but in industries where 'right first time' can make or break the deal, you only get one chance. Translation is one such industry, and at Technicolor we had a century's reputation for delivering sparkling brilliance to uphold. It would have been easy to view the translation department as an afterthought in a massive, highly innovative company like Technicolor, where even the company name means 'fabulous visuals', but such was its commitment to perfection, we were afforded the same royal treatment as everyone else.

My company, GoLocalise, is clearly not as big as Technicolor (yet), but almost everything I do today in my business is based on what I learned there. Good translation, or more specifically 'localisation', is about taking one idea and adapting it into another culture or scenario. In a sense, that is what I did by adapting a well-managed global business strategy into a bulletproof small business operational ethos – and it works.

There is no point in reinventing the wheel, and my advice to people entering this marketplace for the first time would be to let the wheel carry you along.

Language is full of flair, romance and possibility, but communication needs to be precise. When you are delivering work for your clients, don't just do a good job, **do a perfect job**. It sounds obvious I know, but that little bit of extra care, attention to detail and determination to get the job right first time will make you stand out from the rest, I promise.

WORDS: Translation interlude

There is an expression in English that people use to describe moments when coincidence seems to be working at its impressive best to bring about the most unexpected of circumstances. Perhaps you are talking to someone you have just met and, as the conversation develops, you discover that your parents grew up in the same small village in Andalucía. Or you walk out of a shop while on holiday in Australia, bump into an old school friend and utter those time-honoured magical words: 'It's a small world.'

What is interesting about this phrase is that it has, in recent times, taken on an additional meaning. We now use it as an observation of the way that technology seems to have shrunk the world, or in reality brought us all a whole lot closer together within it. With worldwide communication in an instant, intercontinental trading commonplace, and global travel often easier than it is inside your own country, we truly do live in 'a small world'.

Yet it is still easy for the largest of global brands and international corporations to make mega mistakes in translation. Here are a few of my favourite (almost Freudian) commercial foul-ups:

- 'Nothing sucks like an Electrolux'. When the Swedish vacuum cleaner manufacturer decided to launch its products in the USA, technically there was nothing wrong with their slogan. Suck does mean to remove the air from a confined space, to create a vacuum that will draw in dust and fluff, and of course their intention was to suggest that their products performed this action better than the market's alternatives. If only their researchers had looked into American-English a little further, they'd have seen that 'to suck' to Americans means to be rubbish (rather than to clean it up).

- 'Come alive with the Pepsi generation'. Urban myth, with an element of truth, has it that when Pepsi used this slogan in the 1960s it caused quite a spooky stir in China, or at least it suggested that the sugary drink might cause a stir among the undead. The literal translation of this phrase implied that Pepsi had the power to bring dead ancestors back to life, a claim that apparently caused offence and confusion in equal measure.

  As a possible consequence of that error, the global drinks giant has never quite beaten its eternal rival, Coca-Cola, to the number one spot in that part of the world, although it is interesting to note that in some Chinese dialects the phonetic pronunciation of Coca-Cola, 'Ke-kou-Ke-la', can be understood as 'bite the wax tadpole'. Clearly wax models of baby frogs are more palatable than the idea of resurrection.

- 'Assume nothing'. HSBC currently uses the tagline 'The world's local bank', with the emphasis being that they provide a local service where they understand different cultures. Most of their advertising is built around this philosophy and the claim that they make no assumptions about individuals' circumstances. The idea of 'assuming nothing' seemed like a smart one to the marketing gurus who first started to play with it in 2009. What could possibly go wrong with a two-word slogan that encapsulated a global banking giant's worldwide philosophy? It was brilliant.

They quickly hit a problem – they had made a big assumption. No one had checked what the translation might be in all of the different countries, especially the local areas which were the very markets HSBC was aiming to impress. In many languages (major and minor ones), the phrase was translated as 'do nothing', which is probably not a particularly good message from a forward-thinking, progressive local bank.

Back to Technicolor and the way in which they made translation, and localisation in particular, work well throughout the global entertainments industry.

Working for such a great company at the top of its game taught me about the power of being bulletproof. That's why, even though I was only there for a short while, Technicolor was the pot of gold at the end of the rainbow. My time there taught me as much about business as I'd learned in the previous twenty years, and most of it was down to people like my manager at the time, Stewart Dickison (more about him later).

Seeing a smooth operation, where everyone knew their place and worked well together, offered me a great role model for when I set up my own business. Suppliers were looked after and managed, clients were provided for, and the staff were afforded respect for the contributions they made. I learned about pricing, paying suppliers and making a margin – essential lessons that I am amazed a lot of small business owners don't seem to understand.

There were also a multitude of other details that, because I had begun developing my obsession with being bulletproof, I picked up. I wasn't consciously storing up skills for a future life as an entrepreneur, but maybe the seed of that idea had been planted. I learned how to write an email effectively as an internal communication, a supplier instruction or as part of important customer care. I observed the way the better managers dealt with staff who had stepped out of line and needed some gentle (or even forceful) cajoling back on side. This is a priceless skill because human nature is to take advantage of a favourable circumstance (or working environment) and push the boundaries of reasonable behaviour, and I am so glad I recognised this back then, because getting the right balance in the human behaviour stakes creates a place where everyone can excel.

LESSON: Good practice translates into great results

Throughout my life, and particularly in my business life, I have become an observer of behaviours and the results of those behaviours in other people. To me, it makes perfect sense that if one course of action leads to a great result, and another leads to a poor or mediocre result, you'd choose the first, yet there is a big difference between 'knowing' and 'knowing and doing'. My advice to anyone wanting to be successful in business is to become a student of good practice, then follow and apply that same good practice. It seems such an obvious thing to say, but I see so many people ignore the obvious and misapply answers that are right in front of their eyes.

When I was studying, I was taught lessons in a classroom, including theory, written tests and listening to the teachers. Don't get me wrong, the facts and rules they instilled in me were invaluable (no one could do any type of technical job without having been educated in it), but it was getting out there and using my skills which made all the difference for me. Combining the performing of a technical task with the human element of interaction and personality gave it life; being part of a team and seeing the difference that commitment made when up against apathy showed its substance; and understanding how appreciation of your part in the whole is a far more powerful motivator than being treated like an animal in a cage became the cornerstone of everything.

Life lessons such as these are the key to success – not just seeing them, but believing in them and making them part of the way you run your business and life. That is why my time at Technicolor lit up and painted a spectral array of opportunity onto the canvas of my world.

Then, late in 2006, after just eighteen months in my dream job, I was made redundant. It's funny how things like that always happen when everything seems too perfect, and of course nothing lasts forever, but it was like Technicolor had pulled the plug out of the pool in the paradise where I had been swimming. I felt as though the rain had started to fall again, but the sun was hidden behind a big black cloud, and the rainbow had gone with it. In actual fact, the company had been called back to America. The dollar was weak against the pound at that time, there wasn't as much work available in the European market, and it wasn't a viable option to keep the London office running.

Even in this there was an opportunity for me to learn and grow, and by that time I had seen enough to know that all I had to do was to keep working hard at making the next opportunity come along. I reached for my chorizo sandwiches, and the familiar taste of home helped reassure me that there was no way I was going to sit and wait for something happen.

Around fifty people were made redundant from the London office, and because of the reputation that the company had, it wasn't long before most of us were back in the sunshine. I had to reach for my shades in less than a week, when another audiovisual company, VisionText, made me an offer. I had my redundancy money and a new role doing much the same job for a competitor, but it was never quite as good. I'd had a taste of the right way to do things, and lesser fruit just wouldn't satisfy anymore. It had to be the right way or no way at all for me, so I knew this was only ever going to be a short-term fix.

At one point, I talked of moving to America with Technicolor, but I realised I had fallen in love with England, so there was only one option left – I would build my own version of the perfect place to work. The rude awakening of redundancy had pushed me towards what I now see as the place where I was always destined to be – setting up my own business and doing things my way. I felt like my purpose was calling (although I was a little bit afraid) and I was at last going to create my own sunshine.

Little did I know that there was going to be a whole lot of trying to push water uphill with a rake before I would finally get to the beach. The sunlounger, tanning cream and piña coladas would have to wait a little longer.

The next stage of the story might get a little messy, so here are a few more idioms to chew on before I move on.

WORDS: Translation interlude

'Pushing water uphill with a rake' is one of those sayings which needs no explanation. It is abundantly clear in any language – as long as you know what a rake is – but if you are still in any doubt, it means putting in a lot of effort while feeling like you are getting nowhere.

That one is clear, but here are a few phrases, or idioms, from different countries that have little meaning, bizarre connotations or may even cause offence across the language border. Occasionally these sayings are so antiquated and twisted by time that even in their native country their origin is a matter of sheer guesswork, and this is particularly true of the Mother Tongue of Great Britain, with her colourful, diverse and multicultural history, shaped by centuries of invasion, congregation and civil war. If you are one of the 6% of the world's population who speaks English as a first language, rest assured that you are not alone in littering your vocabulary with untranslatable sayings.

Here are a few of my favourites for you to enjoy and share with your friends:

- In Germany, if someone is totally oblivious to the things going on around them, they are said to 'have tomatoes on their eyes'.

The exact origins of the phrase are uncertain, but the most popular theory is that the person is red-eyed from having stayed up too late the night before, which would account for them being unable to concentrate on the here and now and missing things that are clear to everyone else. Who knows the real origin? Maybe it was simply a description of someone who used to miss things because they insisted on wearing sunglasses made of tomatoes, although I think the first idea is probably more likely.

- Sometimes idioms that don't translate literally do have equivalents in other languages. In English, if a person is born into a rich family and is unaware of what it means to work hard or go without, they might be described as 'having been born with a silver spoon in their mouth'. This saying originated in the 1700s when the aristocracy would bring their own cutlery to dinner rather than risk facing the ignominy of a lesser spoon. Over time, it became a symbol of status to carry a silver spoon

around, indicating that the holder was a person of property or wealth.
- Interestingly, an old Spanish proverb, quoted in the famous novel *Don Quixote*,[6] says, *'muchas veces donde hay estacas no hay tocinos'*. Literally translated, this means 'often where there are hooks there are no hams' in reference to hooks that a butcher would hang hams on, but in a 1719 English version of the novel this line was translated as 'tis not all gold that glisters, and every man not born with a silver spoon in his mouth'.[7] Those readers more familiar with English idioms will recognise another here (all that glitters is not gold), but it is interesting that the silver spoon reference has little to do with the original meaning. For hundreds of years, translators of literature have been wrestling with meanings being lost in translation and, as a result, have often mixed their idioms.
- Incidentally, in Swedish there is an even more delightful (if slightly fishy) way of expressing the idea of a pampered upbringing. The Swedes say that the fortunate person dwelling in the lap of luxury must have 'slid in on a shrimp sandwich'. I'm not sure if this refers to the slippery nature of shellfish in general, or maybe that shrimps were something of an upper-class delicacy back in the day in Sweden, but either way, I like this one.

---

6 Cervantes, M, *Don Quixote* (Penguin, 2002)
7 Cervantes, M, *The History of the Renowned Don Quixote de la Mancha, 4: In four volumes* (Peter Motteux, 1719), https://books.google.co.uk/books?id=WVSPbb_sBbwC&pg=PA345&redir_esc=y#v=onepage&q&f=false

- The Russians have many quirky sayings too, some of which have changed over time because of changes in language. One that caught my attention is '*veshat lapshu na ushi*', which roughly translated means 'to hang noodles on someone's ears'.

  The closest equivalent in English would be to 'pull the wool over someone's eyes', meaning to try and get the better of someone, mislead them or trick them. Apparently, the wool in the English version refers to a judge's wig, the imagery suggesting that his woollen wig is pulled down in front of his eyes to block out his vision – or insight. While there is a similar feel to the two phrases, there is little logic behind the idea of noodle-induced confusion. It does create quite a funny image in your mind, though.

CHANCING YOUR ARM

> When you understand that the Russian word *lapsha* can mean both noodles and scraps of cloth, it begins to make a little more sense. Perhaps it relays the idea of causing temporary deafness by covering the ears and muffling the sound around them, but whatever the original intent, the noodle meaning of the word tends to be used today and builds an amusing picture for those who see it from a foreigner's viewpoint.

I hope that you have enjoyed this latest little journey into untranslatable idioms. Next, I am going to tell you how I branched out into running a business for myself, which was another uphill chapter full of lessons to learn in my life.

5
The Hard Road And The Freeloader

Some people are determined to make things happen in their life, and they work hard to achieve their goals. Others seem convinced that life owes them their goals, and working hard might get in the way.

In 2006 I went into partnership with a German guy I had previously worked with, to set up voxHouse. He was an experienced voice-over talent who was brilliant at doing just that – laying down tracks for projects. I had been doing some work as a voice-over artist myself while working at VisionText, and my portfolio at the time included projects with The Discovery Channel, Nickelodeon and Cartoon Network. It had been good to get back in front of a mic and record work for some exciting projects. Studying hadn't been as much fun (well, maybe some of the extra-curricular activity was), and my experience of work had introduced me to both the best and the worst it could be, but this felt great and gave me a sense of freedom again. I even spent a bit of time as the voice of Paco Rabanne – now that was definitely worth writing home about. Sales of that particular fragrance had never been so high in Gijón.

Between us, my German business partner and I had the skills and the knowledge to deliver some first-class results. I also had a database of voice-over talent that I had acquired and learned to trust (especially the bulletproof ones) during the previous years, so everything was in place and perfectly positioned for voxHouse to become an awesome localisation business.

It had one fatal flaw – miscommunication.

At the time, I thought the problem lay solely with my business partner, but looking back I can see clearly that we were just too different. Often different is good – the easily translatable expression 'two sides of the same coin' describes the benefits of two approaches, ideas or personalities coming together to create a useful and valuable asset, but sometimes different means just that – opposing views, intentions, desires and methods. In the end, one cancels the other out and ultimately destroys the chances of success, or even the relationship altogether.

Unfortunately, it was the latter extreme of different which influenced us most of all.

Before I go on, I know it is accepted practice in the world of celebrities and big business to name and shame old colleagues, but it is not my way. While I have a more considered view of the reason for the business's failure now, it is still a painful recollection, so my former business partner shall remain nameless in this book because that is the right thing to do. Some of the detail needs to come out, though.

As with all these things, the business started with us sitting down and discussing our strategy for the company. We went through our personal objectives and targets, the direction we wanted the business to go, and the ultimate goal for its future – the proverbial five-year plan. We agreed all the way, found common ground, big ambitions, promises of commitment and the ensuing excitement of a new venture with all the right ingredients to make magic happen, but despite the nods and affirmations, we'd totally misunderstood each other's goals and intentions.

I departed from our first meeting with the wind in my sails, intending to build a business with lots of exciting customers, an artillery of bulletproof voice-over talent, efficient internal processes, a premium-service offering and a fabulous working environment. From the same meeting, my partner believed he was just going to be doing more freelance voice-over work himself and perhaps outsourcing a bit on the side. Amazing.

> **LESSON: The key to good business practice is to keep practising good business**
>
> I've often wondered how two translation and communication experts could fail to understand each other to such a gargantuan degree. The result of that, and many subsequent miscommunications in the two and a half years that followed, was fatal for our business and almost ruined every good belief that I had discovered up to that point.
>
> In business, as in life, the single most important skill to master is good communication. Become great at selling, be an understanding boss, create products that fit your customers' needs, and demonstrate a work ethic that will inspire everyone around you, but most of all communicate what you mean and work hard to understand what others mean.
>
> It is ironic that I work in the translation industry, and there is a close correlation between translation and sharing meaning. My business is all about the former, but all business depends on the latter. In fact, the quality of all relationships, in any walk of life, is massively enhanced through the power of clear communication.
>
> How is yours?

I got committed, putting in eighteen-hour days, securing clients, creating marketing materials, making things happen behind the scenes, finding talent and investing in systems. To be fair, my business partner spent six months making our website look absolutely perfect (note the sarcastic tone), but that meant the business was without one partner for the whole time he was tinkering. It drove me to despair. The only time he showed any interest in the company at all was when I found a new client who needed German voice-over work, so in a sense I became a customer to my business partner, and not one that he was looking after or appreciating much. That's how it felt to me, anyway.

Sometimes in business you need to show a ruthless streak. I mentioned earlier that the right thing to do is not to mention the name of my previous business partner, and I stand by that decision, but dissolving the business was *definitely* the right thing to do. The only mistake I made was letting it drag on so long, putting up with our differences for two and a half years. You know that scenario when you realise pretty much as soon as you have made a decision that it is the wrong one? Well, this was one of those times, and if you ever find yourself in a similar place, my advice would be to take action sooner rather than later. It will save you a lot of pain in the long run.

As much as I wanted to take the business forward and turn it into something akin to the great examples

I had seen elsewhere, my partner was determined to keep it ticking over. He didn't hear my initially timid but progressively stronger suggestions that we go our separate ways: as far as he was concerned, the business was a source of freelance work (the aforementioned 'customer') for him, so why would he want it to stop? Eventually, I decided to take the only course of action left to me, and I began to put any new business into a brand-new company. This one was going to be mine, fuelled by my passion, run on my terms under my rules. In some ways, I felt a little guilty doing this without telling him, but hand on heart I can say I had tried being forthright and reasonable. Eventually it hurt too much to bear.

As voxHouse's order book got thinner and thinner, it became obvious to my partner (at last) that there was no longer a business to argue about, and the end was finally in sight. The crunch arrived and we settled on a deal which meant I could buy my way out of the partnership, but it was a painful moment. I was not just parting with a large sum of money; I had ploughed my heart and soul into the opportunity, and for a while I'd believed in it.

> **LESSON: Sometimes you need to find your roar**
>
> This episode in my career was probably one of the lowest points. It affected me deeply, and even recalling the events of that time brings back the emotion, but, as with so many of life's trials, it taught me a lot about

> myself. I realised that everyone is different and you cannot change who you are (nor should you have to), but I would encourage you to cultivate the fighter within you. You will almost certainly need it at some point.
>
> If you are someone who knows me personally, then I hope that you think of me as a good-natured, friendly and happy sort of person. If you have seen me in adversity, under pressure or in ambitious mode, then you will also know me to be quite determined, a little bit maverick and certainly a risk-taker. I'm not telling you this as a kind of egotistical rant, I promise, but because it matters. If you want to be successful in life or business, you cannot do it by being nice all of the time. You do not need to be cruel or dishonest (I despise those qualities), but you do need to be prepared to take on your challenges. If that involves rolling up your sleeves and getting dirty, or jumping in at the deep end (without armbands) from time to time, then go for it.
>
> Your passion-fuelled enthusiasm might even get you into trouble sometimes, and you will make the odd mistake here and there, but if you pick yourself up each time and keep fighting, there will always be a place for the nice guy to come and mop up the mess. My big lesson here was to be a lion, not a coward, and to develop an unswerving eagle eye when it comes to chasing down my dreams.

With that in mind, and before we move on to the next episode in my story, here are a few animal-related untranslatables to make you think a little.

CHANCING YOUR ARM

WORDS: Translation interlude

'*Pagar o pato*' is a Portuguese saying that comes from a traditional game where the loser has to pay for a duck – presumably one that he doesn't want. It basically means to 'pay the consequences for something that was not your fault', but the literal translation is 'pay the duck'. Imagine having to translate that one.

Similar to the Portuguese duck idiom, but slightly weirder and requiring even more explanation, is the Swedish expression '*att bära hundhuvudet*'. The literal translation into English is 'to carry the dog's head', and it means the same thing – to take the blame for something that has gone horribly wrong. Its origins date back to medieval Germany where a punishment for small misdemeanours among the upper classes was humiliation. One method was to make the culprit carry a dog in their arms while walking through a public place. Another variation on this penance would be for them to wear a dog's head on a rope around their neck. Cruel, really, especially for the dog who was the one paying the duck on that occasion.

Interestingly, both of these idioms could be replaced with a single word that describes another animal that took the blame, and this example is one of the oldest in the world, dating back to the days of the Old Testament when early Jewish priests sacrificed the innocent 'scapegoat' to cover for the sins of the people.

Let me finish this section with something a little more light-hearted, otherwise you might think I'm still trying to lay the blame for the failure of voxHouse on my erstwhile business partner.

In Poland, people use an expression '*Słoń nastąpił ci na ucho?*' which translates in English as 'Did an elephant stomp on your ear?' This is a fairly dramatic way of suggesting that the recipient of the comment has no musical taste, and the mind boggles with the pictures that this might paint for people trying to translate it. A similar Croatian accusation is probably easier to explain, but only after you have stopped laughing. '*Pjevaš kao da ti je slon prdnuo u uho*' means 'you sing like an elephant farted in your ear'.

Now it's time to tune in to the story again.

One of the good things to come out of the voxHouse episode was that I learned how to be a sound engineer. Prior to that, I had learned all about the business side of things and channelled my natural winning mentality into getting new customers, but being an owner-manager, I felt as though it was my duty to understand every aspect of the business I was running. This was useful later on when I came to employ full-time staff to do things for me, as I have always found that the way to get the best out of other people is to understand what it is you expect of them, and for them to know that you understand. Mutual ground is always a firm place upon which to stand when building relationships.

At last I was fully prepared for the next chapter – the one that ticked all the boxes of a dream that had started as a child's hazy imagining over twenty years earlier. Armed with big business experience (the best and the worst of it), technical ability, a desire to win new business and an insatiable natural desire, I stepped up to the mark. Having tasted success and overcome adversity, I had identified exactly what my dream looked like, so with laser-focused clarity, belief and determination I took the biggest step of my life. I did it all on my own.

Note: If you read that last paragraph and thought to yourself, *Steady on, David – that all sounds a bit romantic and grandiose*, then thank you for noticing. This was one of the biggest moments of my life and a key factor in how I got to be where I am now: a multi-award-winning, successful and highly respected entrepreneur. I am proud of where I am today and how I got here, and there is a big lesson in this for you too, especially if you are just starting out on your business journey and working out what your dream looks like.

> ### LESSON: You have to believe in yourself
>
> If you do not **believe in yourself**, it is certain that no one else will. When I say I am proud of what I have achieved, it is not done in a self-centred, big-headed way. I know this because today I surround myself with brilliant entrepreneurs whom I trust to tell me the truth and whose opinions I have also learned to trust. Some of their comments and quotes are included in this book, all of them are successful leaders and innovators in their individual areas of expertise, and I have learned from them that having pride in your achievement is essential to reach even greater goals. Remembering your successes and failures is paramount to improving the way that you get there.

> My purpose in finishing the chapter in this way is to encourage you, because if you are just starting out in business, or you have reached a crossroads in your life and need some inspiration, then I know you can do it. If a simple lad from a small Spanish town with an eclectic upbringing, a propensity for mischief and no formal business education can achieve his goals, then so can you. If I can move to a new country, with a foreign, often strange, culture and language, and create my own version of what I see as success, then you must be able to do the same.

Now let me introduce you to GoLocalise and the next chapter in my story. After that, I am going to share some experiences and lessons about living, working and being successful in a foreign country.

6
Long Days, More Learning And GoLocalise

In 2008 I set up GoLocalise, doing it my way. For the first time, I was able to find the clients I wanted, use the talent that I trusted and make hard work and determination the foundation of all I did. The company was going to become bulletproof, and that meant collecting together the best linguists and voice-over talents I had met over the years leading up to that point.

From day one, I wanted GoLocalise to stand out for delivering reliable and consistent quality, but I had to start with another skill that I had practised and knew well. I started spamming again.

By the way, I do not advocate spamming as a good way of marketing. At the time, it was the only thing I knew, and I still wasn't aware that there was anything unethical or illegal in what I was doing. I only kept up the campaign for a few months – enough to get the business going in the first place. In today's market it is easier and more effective to build a highly engaged, fully subscribed list – and that is what I now do, just for the record.

Like the first time round, I got a mixed response to my spamming. Some people hated me for it, and a few phone calls were littered with unrepeatable language as they expressed their displeasure. Others responded more kindly, and some of the recipients already knew about me, so I won a few trial orders. The key, though, was that I had learned a few lessons over the years, and one in particular that made a massive difference was that I knew how to write a good email. It was relevant in that it addressed a problem I knew would be familiar to my ideal customers; it was well positioned because I understood their market and could demonstrate credibility; and finally, it was persuasive because I gave them an offer that would be hard to resist.

Those who ignored my emails or got upset with me weren't destined to be my customers. I had learned to accept that, and while I would have preferred to avoid the verbal abuse, at least I knew where I stood. It was a win-win with those who responded positively. They clearly saw that GoLocalise could offer them something that they weren't getting elsewhere, so all I had to do was deliver, and I was fortunate enough to have built a team of bulletproof translators, subtitlers and voice-over talent that I knew would deliver on my marketing promises.

> **LESSON: Success in business is simple**
>
> Identify a hungry crowd (people who have a need) and communicate to them that you have the solution. Then go and feed their need at a cost that they deem to be good value. (As a proviso here, it is important to identify that 'good value' should never mean the same thing as 'cheap'. Quality is always worth paying for, as long as it genuinely represents value for money.)
>
> The final part of the easiest jigsaw in the world is to do the job consistently well. That way your customers will love you and continue to use you forever (or at least as long as they have a need). The only caveat I would add to this simplified view of success in business is that you need to work hard, **believe in yourself** and be brave enough to have a go.

One of the great things I did from the first days of GoLocalise (looking back, I might even say it was inspired) was to offer our services at higher rates than most. If I'm honest (which I try to be), this wasn't done because I knew it was a good marketing strategy, nor was I aware that premium rates attract better customers; it was done because in my previous roles – managing large translation projects – I had come to hate negotiating rates with my bulletproof suppliers. I always wanted to use the best talent, and that meant valuing the expertise, delivery and commitment those people brought to the project. Having to start each engagement with an uncomfortable discussion about reduced payments was never the best motivator.

The most valuable relationships in business are multidirectional – the customers are happy, the supplier is happy and their suppliers are happy. GoLocalise, with little market presence, no trading track record and parading an above-average pricing structure, set off to conquer the world. To supplement the email marketing, I went out and did a bit of face-to-face networking (with limited success), and I followed up everything on the phone. I instinctively knew if I could persuade a few people to give me a chance, I could turn them into believers.

As soon as we got a new customer on board, whether it was the result of an email or a conversation on the phone, we always delivered. Over time the word got out (translated into different languages, of course) and soon people started ringing us. One such referral phone call led to our largest customer coming on board – a company that went on to spend over half a million pounds in six years and is still using us today.

When I say GoLocalise was not the cheapest in the marketplace, it is important to note that often we could save our customers money because we listened to their requirements and offered them a solution rather than a product.

> **LESSON: Off-the-shelf means products and off-the-back-of-a-conversation means solutions**
>
> The difference between a solution and a product is simple. A customer came to us one day with a large project which required ten different voices. All the competitors' quotes (they later told us) were comprised of ten actors doing the different parts. Each sent their proposal in print, and the only differentiator was the cost per voice.
>
> We called the customer and discussed what they required. Some of the parts were significantly smaller than others and we knew a lot of talented voice-over artists, so we pitched an offer to the customer at a higher rate per actor which only required four artists. Each talent was capable of delivering different voices, and we sent the client examples of their capabilities. Our customer got a high-quality result, we won credibility and earned our percentage, and all of our suppliers earned a rate that was worthy of their ability.

I mentioned earlier that I had taught myself to be a sound engineer, using tools such as Pro Tools and Audition, but in the early days of GoLocalise it didn't stop there. In the same way that I was determined to provide bulletproof localisation talent, I also wanted the back-office environment to work perfectly, which meant becoming the project manager, sales manager, accounts manager and occasional sound engineer. While this was partly economy-driven to keep the costs down, I was determined not to leave anything to chance when it came to delivery, but ultimately this could not continue. There are only so many eighteen-hour days that even the most committed of bodies can take. If I'd carried on too long, I may well have ended up being 'committed' myself.

An important part of the transition from a one-man band to a team, albeit supported by an army of bulletproof talent, was to document my processes. This meant writing down all the good practices I had developed while doing the roles myself, then, as I employed people full-time, I handed them the manual. Again, this was something that I didn't really think through; it just turned out to be an excellent way of setting a standard for others to follow.

Within a few years, just when the long days were starting to get the better of me, I took on my first full-time member of staff, and although it wasn't an easy path, I was eventually able to build a bulletproof in-house team. I spent a huge amount of money developing a tailor-made back-office system (called FileMaker), which automated almost every process we needed. It was, and to this day probably still is, one of the best investments the business has ever made.

I will come back to the process of moving from working alone to becoming a business employing people in a later chapter. Having arrived at the idea of hiring people, I'd like to share a few of my favourite people-related untranslatable idioms.

WORDS: Translation interlude

In 1987 Pope John Paul II visited Miami in Florida. Merchandising companies all over the area worked flat out to capitalise on the historic visit and sell their wares. One T-shirt maker, not wanting to miss out on the multicultural opportunities, had 'I saw the Pope' shirts made, translating the slogan into a variety of languages, but a tiny error on the Latin American one reduced the spiritual leader of the Catholic Church to an earthly position. Instead of the correct '*El Papa*' the slogan read '*La Papa*', suggesting that the wearer had seen 'the potato'.

The same year, a small American airline, Braniff Airlines, started promoting the fact that all of its flights were super luxurious with the line 'Fly in leather'. This clearly referred to the seats, but the Spanish translation, '*Vuela en cuero*', meant 'Fly naked' – a slightly different connotation than the intended one.

This next one could have started a religious war, and had it gone ahead it would have instantly alienated at least half an entire population. In 1994 the telecoms company Orange had just launched its now-familiar slogan, 'The future's bright, the future's Orange'. Fortunately, a politically aware employee noted that this might not go down too well in Northern Ireland, where there is a strong loyalist Protestant movement called the Orange Order. For a company to have hung its brand on a promise that a bright future would come in the shape of one of the two major religious factions in Northern Ireland would have been commercial suicide among the Catholics.

Imagine you have friends over to visit from Hungary, partly because they want to practise their English. While you are sitting in the living room after dinner on the first evening, the travel is clearly catching up with their child and he starts to get fidgety. The parents suggest that he go to bed, which turns the restlessness into tears, and then one of them says, 'Why are you giving drinks to the mice?'

You look around to see if Harry the Hamster has escaped or the cat has brought in a little present again, and your quizzical looks lead your guests to explain that is just what people say in Hungary when kids cry.

OK, so maybe there is some logic there. Mice live on the ground and that is typically where tears fall, so potentially they could drink the tears, but sometimes phrases have no decipherable explanation or origin. In Poland, for example, when someone is daydreaming, it is said that they are 'thinking of blue almonds'. While I like the sound of this and there is a somewhat romantic connotation, it does not make any sense.

There is a lesson in the idea that, like languages, people are not always the easiest things to understand and translate into our own mindset. One of the running themes throughout my story is the idea of being bulletproof, but on the reverse side, some people are just too fragile and, as a result, unreliable. Don't get me wrong here, I know plenty of people whose life and health circumstances are challenging, and I am certainly not referring to them – I have nothing but the highest regard for people who face whatever life throws at them and keep going regardless. I'm referring to the people who can become bulletproof, but for whatever reason don't. They are the ones who can hold back success and open up your business to a volley of bullets from which it has no defence. My advice would be to avoid them in the first place.

If you are trying to build a business, and you need to employ people to go on that journey with you, make sure you find ones with the same heart. I place this quality far above technical ability: it sits right up there with doing your best every time. In the same way that I learned who were my bulletproof voice-over talents and gave them the majority of the work, especially the good jobs, I found out about staff the hard way.

I don't want to go into too much detail here (I will reveal more in a later chapter); suffice to say that previous experience can help make sure that you pay more attention when hiring people in the future. I would like to mention that my current team are all fantastic.

LESSON: Get good at being good

A big lesson for translators. When I was a child, it was the romance, fluidity and unexpected within languages which attracted me. I loved the fact that stories and the use of different words in different cultures could take you on journeys to imaginary places and unknown worlds. It was the flexibility of the rules that caught my heart. In those days, I hated the exactness of science. The idea of maths equations would make me lose sleep at night, and the severity of the white-coated teachers made me shiver.

I still love the beauty of linguistics and the ability to express yourself and understand the culture of conversation, but I have come to learn that to be a success in the world of translation and localisation, you must embrace perfection too. Attention to detail is paramount. You need to be fussy with everything and treat it like a science. Whether it is choosing the exact word or the right intonation of the pronunciation in a voice-over, the extra attention makes all the difference.

If you want to become a bulletproof voice-over talent or translator, please get good at being good. Do not oversell yourself to start with; begin at the bottom and prove yourself. Do not settle for the first take or the turn-up-and-record approach; do your research, practise, pay attention and make sure that every time you deliver some work it is the best that it can be. I promise you this will get you noticed and on the road to fulfilling your ambitions.

The other general lesson here is that people can change. My natural tendency was to daydream (think of blue almonds), go with the flow and get carried away

> with the fun of language. After meeting people who inspired me (at places like Technicolor) and learning that attention to detail matters, I made myself change. I have seen other people, in many different industries, dedicate themselves to changing their natural behaviour because they wanted to be better. Because of that, I am convinced that anyone who wants to change can.

In Part Three we will delve into the true mind and activity of an entrepreneur. Up until this point, I'd been playing at it really, but this is when I got serious. I will reveal some of the secrets that helped me find my way to winning multiple awards, highlight a few more of the dangers, and share some of the wisdom that I learned. Whatever your goals and dreams, I sincerely hope that my experiences can help you achieve them.

Firstly, I think it would be good for you to meet some genuinely bulletproof friends of mine.

PART THREE
LEND ME YOUR EARS FOR A WHILE

7
Friends, Colleagues, Covid And Change

Throughout this book, I have talked about the concept of being bulletproof, and here I'd like to introduce five of the people I have come to think of as being just that. The first three are colleagues from the early days of my business. They represent different countries, cultures, skills and personalities but have one major thing in common – they quickly became firm friends of mine because I learned I could totally rely on them. The fourth and fifth bulletproof characters became important later in the story. Their work helped me make a mental shift from being a busy hardworking entrepreneur to the more settled business owner you see before you today.

At the start, of course, I was in a position where I wanted my business to do well and it was important for me to work with people I could trust. I knew whatever we delivered to the customer had to be outstanding. My emphasis was not just on winning customers, but also on keeping them. I felt that if our output wasn't good enough, we would immediately lose out by not getting repeat orders. The following people played a huge part in ensuring that, in our early days, we avoided that problem.

Deborah Chan: The grand master of Asian linguistics

I met Deborah when I was working as a project manager for Technicolor back in 2004. From the first job I engaged her in (she already came highly recommended), she became my top choice for any work requiring Chinese.

The thing to remember with translation is that it is often only the end-user customer who can tell you if the work is any good, and that means after the event. Unless you speak the language in question, you have no way of knowing until feedback arrives, and often you only get that if there is a problem. It was that rarest of features, unsolicited positive feedback, which highlighted Deborah's excellence to me. After her first job, my customer said her work was flawless, which is not a word many people would use lightly. They even went on to suggest that her work was better than the original version, and in translation that makes it amazing.

What stands out about Deborah is that, since that first job, she has been consistently flawless. In the ten-plus years that I have been giving her work, I can genuinely say that I have never had a complaint or any cause for concern. Her attention to detail is second to none, her in-depth knowledge of the languages she translates is comprehensive and her attitude is a joy to be around. That in a nutshell sums up perhaps the most important aspect of being bulletproof: being 100% reliable. It involves far more than simply being talented (which Deborah clearly is); it also means that a person cares about the work and is diligent about giving the best result, time after time.

In terms of work requiring talent and ability, there is no shortage for Deborah. She translates, subtitles, teaches, lectures at UCL and even works as a voice-over talent and world-class interpreter, and not just in a single language – she is fluent in Cantonese and Mandarin (spoken in Mainland China, Taiwan and Hong Kong) and has perfect English, both spoken and written.

Her portfolio is amazing, and includes work for the BBC and global companies such as BP, GlaxoSmith-Kline, Microsoft, Hewlett-Packard, McAfee, HSBC and Shell. She even worked on the successful London 2012 Olympic bid. A clever person indeed.

> **LESSON: Being flawless and becoming bulletproof**
>
> I have got to know many excellent translators and voice-over talents during my time in the industry. Few are technically as good as Deborah, but it is not that which makes her stand out from the crowd.

> I know that whenever I give her a project, it will be finished with care, attention, integrity and ultimately with perfection. That is why I see her as flawless, why I chose her as one of the people to represent this rare breed in my book, and why I think of her as bulletproof.
>
> If you are looking to get into translation or any other area of business, then I would urge you to follow her example. People will notice if you are consistently seen to be reliable, just as much as they will remember if you are not. They will see you as the safest option, be prepared to pay more for your services, and talk about you to people they know. If you happen to be the best at what you do, you are on to a winner.

You may have heard of my next bulletproof friend from the early days. If you have children, then you definitely will have. Maybe not heard of him exactly, but you'll certainly have heard his voice.

Javier Fernandez-Peña: The voice that goes to infinity and beyond (via Spain)

I had been aware of Javier for many years before I met him, because he is well known in the industry. He famously recorded the voice of the Spanish Buzz Lightyear in *Toy Story 3*, playing the part in the movie when the other toys accidentally reset him. It is hilarious and I'd advise you to go and watch it if you haven't already. This job, alongside a lot of other highly prestigious work, has earned him the nickname among his English colleagues of 'The Voice of Spain'.

Although I didn't know him at the time, we grew up in a similar part of Spain and share many memories of the same places from our childhoods. Javier comes from Oviedo, the town where I gained my work experience at Radio Vetusta, and he may even have listened to my show occasionally. It was through a friend of a friend that I first used Javier for work, and it was great to see someone with a reputation to live up to. His performance was immaculate and took the idea of professionalism to another level. This is the difference between the star player in a local football team and Cristiano Ronaldo, or someone who considers themselves to be a good fast driver and Lewis Hamilton.

The mixture of natural talent, years of experience and a commitment to continually improving his art makes Javier stand out, which makes him bulletproof. He is also versatile and can turn his voice to dubbing, e-learning products and corporate recordings – when he is not working on The Discovery Channel and Bloomberg TV.

> **LESSON: Keep going to infinity and beyond**
>
> The bulletproof lesson Javier teaches is to be the best you can be. It is the ultimate acclaim to be recognised as the most sought-after in a particular market, but it doesn't happen overnight, and it won't happen at all if you stop trying. Too many people, not just in this industry but all over the world, give up too soon. Javier has had a long and distinguished career because he has worked hard and developed his talent throughout

> his life. It wasn't until 2010, when *Toy Story 3* came out, that he gained international acclaim, though.
>
> The ultimate success in any business is built on getting good, being diligent, becoming bulletproof and keeping going until the big break arrives. As the great golfer Gary Player used to say, 'The more I practise, the luckier I get.'[8] Javier certainly created his opportunity and good fortune by being 'The Voice of Spain' – the best in the world within his particular niche.

The third bulletproof voice talent that helped me establish the business is similar to Javier, but with a marvellous English accent.

Roland Bearne: The most adaptable, compelling and professional voice in England

I first came across Roland while I was working as a project manager at VisionText, and he stood out because of the scarce specialism that he provided. He was one of the few people in the UK at the time who could write, record and produce audio description materials and content. This was a relatively new thing back then and involved writing scripts which accurately described the visuals on films, providing the nonsighted with access to a descriptive commentary alongside the audio. It was this niche service that brought Roland to my attention, but it was his speaking voice which grabbed it and wouldn't let it go.

---

8   Yocom, G, 'My shot: Gary Player', Golf Digest (12 August 2010), www.golfdigest.com/story/myshot_gd0210, accessed 31 March 2023

He has *the* ultimate English bulletproof voice. It is adaptable, multifaceted, beautifully toned, strong, captivating and always perfectly clear. If you listen to his voice-over demo (and I encourage you to do so), you will hardly believe that all the voices come from the same person, so rich is the variety and tonality of his delivery. Throughout my career, I have not met his equal in voice or style.

As with Deborah and Javier, Roland's skill in being able to deliver an end product is beyond question, but once again, it is not that alone which makes him bulletproof.

Some people have natural talent while others work hard to get to the top. With Roland, I suspect he has a natural flair and ability, but I also believe he has worked hard to perfect his talent. Regardless of whether your ability is the result of having cultivated a gift you were born with or simple determination to turn your passion into a first-class skill, you need other attributes, and the attributes which make the difference with Roland are his confidence, self-belief and application. There is no fuss when he works; he doesn't complicate the role asked of him, he just turns up and nails it. Once again, it is the 100% reliability Roland offers which makes him such an attractive option for companies like GoLocalise.

Another outstanding aspect of Roland's work is his resourcefulness. He has perfected a whole range of accents from within the UK and across many other

English-speaking nations, and he can adapt his delivery to a wide variety of styles.

> **LESSON: Be adaptable when necessary and specific if required**
>
> From a business point of view, there is a lot to be said for specialising in one area and becoming the best at what you do. Roland certainly does that, but, in a competitive world such as the one we live in, you dramatically increase your opportunities if you can provide options. Being flexible and adaptable to your customers' needs is a smart strategy for either businesses or freelancers looking for work. The warning here, though, is only to develop talents and abilities in areas that your customers need. There would be little use in perfecting a Welsh accent if your target market is in Scotland, for example.

Based on the early days of success, I now have hundreds of voice-over talents, translators and other freelance resources available to the business. I am always happy to try new talent, but I have to balance this with doing the right thing for my customers. This means I still value tried, tested and proven bulletproof people like Deborah, Roland and Javier.

Once you know that you're delivering a good service, what next? How do you take a step forward? Eventually, the emphasis for me as a business owner needed to shift from a comfort zone of day-to-day operations to putting my business on a path to sustainable growth and establishing a more concrete future for myself. The help I needed then was around making the business stronger and understanding its value. None of us, however, could have known the Covid-19 pandemic would intervene, and we would all be forced into a more radical change than we ever could have imagined.

It was challenging to run my business during the 2020–2021 lockdowns because we had never worked remotely. We were a small, tightly formed team of ten people at the time. We regularly had people coming into our offices and studios – we would welcome clients and voice-over talents and work with them in person. It was difficult and challenging to move away from what we knew.

The business had no option but to furlough some staff. We needed to keep going as the amount of business from our clients dropped drastically. We didn't go into the red, but it was chaotic. Everything happened at once. I had also just got married too, for goodness' sake. I had planned to move to the USA. I wanted to put myself and my relationship first. Was that fair? Should I park the business or close it entirely? Could I, perhaps, sell it and have some capital to move on to something new? What skills could I draw on? What was I good at? What did I want? I was at a crossroads with lots of questions in the air.

> **LESSON: Sometimes change hits you in the face**
>
> Before 2018 I had not expected to meet my partner or plan a move to the USA. You can read more of that in Chapter 11, but right now I'd like to concentrate on the impact of Covid-19. By the March of 2020, my plans to build a life with my husband had fallen apart. It was clear that world events were beyond our control but that didn't stop immense feelings of frustration. Everything we had planned evaporated and instead of starting a new chapter together we were firmly stuck on two different continents. The change happened incredibly quickly too. Within the space of two weeks, travel arrangements were cancelled and, rather than relocate to Florida, I was destined to stay in London and run my business alone from my apartment. It's easy to look back and forget the lack of concrete information we were given about the pandemic. 'It'll be over by Christmas' quickly turned into next year, for example. To make matters worse, my beloved dog – Rambo – had made the trip ahead of me, leaving me stuck in my apartment truly on my own for the first time in years. To say it was a dark and distressing situation is an understatement, but I powered through one step at a time.

Looking back, if you're looking for what being bulletproof means in action, surviving the pandemic provides countless examples. The question of success isn't always about achieving a set goal or target. Rewards come from how well you react, change direction or bounce back. We all learned this in the years of Covid-19. Everyone has a story about its impacts – lives put on hold, businesses having to re-invent themselves and everyone digging deep.

It is important to reflect on these challenging times and celebrate how resilient we all proved to be. By keeping going, despite immense challenges, life has inevitably returned to some kind of normal.

> **WORDS: Translation interlude**
>
> During the pandemic, I wasn't the only person operating well outside my comfort zone. You could argue that society was as a whole. 'Comfort zone' is one of those phrases that seem to have been around forever but are relatively new. It is also an example of two separate derivations colliding and forming a third common usage. The term 'comfort zone' itself seems to have its roots in the construction industry. It was first used to describe temperature- and humidity-controlled areas. You can imagine reception areas or shared office spaces being described as comfort zones to encourage people to use them. Independently, however, in the early 1900s, a psychologist by the name of Robert Yerkes described the benefits of working at stress levels slightly higher than normal. He created the notion of 'optimal anxiety' and suggested it lay outside a 'zone of comfort'.[9] It took a while for the two concepts to find each other, but now advocating stepping outside one's comfort zone has become commonplace. Like many phrases used in business, the term has become

---

[9] Pietrangelo, A, 'What the Yerkes-Dodson Law says about stress and performance', healthline (22 October 2020), www.healthline.com/health/yerkes-dodson-law, accessed 31 March 2023

> international, with *Komfortzone* being a recognisable, if slightly clumsy, concept to German speakers today. To be truly localised, however, it might be more useful to use a local idiom in translation that covers the same feeling. You might encourage the same German speaker to *spring über deinen schatten*, or jump over their shadow, to try something new instead.

However you phrase it, we learn and grow through reacting to challenging circumstances. Alongside the suppliers who helped me start the business, it feels appropriate to acknowledge two of the people who, while all this was happening, helped me by prompting a shift in mindset and encouraging me to look at my business in a new or different light.

Martin Norbury: The wise, blunt-talking business and accountability coach

Unless you skipped the foreword to this book (in which case go back and read it now), you will already have heard from Martin Norbury. Martin is a business coach and author of *I Don't Work Fridays: Proven strategies to scale your business and not be a slave to it*.[10]

Martin advocates, as an owner, not letting your business drive negative and damaging behaviours. He wants to make sure the world of work works for you as a person. If you want a four-day week, do it. You're

---

10 Norbury, M, *I Don't Work Fridays: Proven strategies to scale your business and not be a slave to it* (Rethink Press, 2016)

the boss. Martin has learned this from working with all kinds of businesses from successful start-ups and multimillion-pound enterprises to family-owned businesses struggling to navigate their futures. As a result, he is full of practical how-to advice and tools you can use to take a business from a good start to long-term sustainable success without sacrificing yourself.

Martin has been working with me at GoLocalise since 2015 and with each interaction, alongside all the business talk, he makes a point of checking in on my happiness and contentment. He'll ask how I am feeling, not just because he's a friendly sort, but also because he knows that's key to running a successful company. If owning a business is not contributing positively to your life, it is time to change something.

With that in mind, one of the things that Martin has consistently said to me over the years is that when you scale a business, you need to be aware of any little cracks. What are the small niggles and frustrations that can sneak in and ruin your mood? As a business expands, problems that initially seem small inconveniences open up and become larger and more troublesome until they're out of control. Martin's most useful contributions to my bulletproof nature include making me link my business success to my wellbeing and helping me realise the true value of ironing out little problems before they become big ones.

Martin was also instrumental in supporting me in understanding that when you own a business, at least in the early days, there are a lot of things that you and you alone know about. Recalling key facts and making quick connections about client relationships and the progress of projects are things that are often needed quickly – and where better to get them from than the boss's brain? This is great when you have your managerial firefighting hat on. You are the living, breathing expert in your business, after all. You can save the day so it's no surprise colleagues come to you for help. The problem is that this information is not always readily accessible if you're not around. If something is not written down in a manual or a database, for example, your team will be left either waiting for your input or having to guess what you'd say or do. I soon realised, again thanks to Martin, that if my brain was the biggest asset in GoLocalise, I immediately cut a large chunk off its functionality whenever I was away from it. This was going to hold back on any growth plans and limit its future.

Thanks to this clever piece of insight, GoLocalise now has a bespoke management system using the FileMaker platform. It acts as a content management system that integrates not only the supplier's and client's databases, but also the leads, quotes, projects and invoices recorded somewhere for the team to access easily. Having the whole thing documented has also helped me view the business above and beyond its people. Our systems and processes are, in themselves, something with value. Talking of value, the other great thing about Martin is he's blunt when it comes to numbers.

> **LESSON: Your business works like an engineering problem**
>
> Even if, like GoLocalise, you're more in the service industry and aren't making tangible physical products, it can help to view your business as a machine with inputs and outputs. Picture a workshop with a series of hoppers, conveyor belts, pulleys, chutes, cogs, levers and so on. Work, in the form of sales leads and potential customers, goes in at one end and revenue and satisfied clients appear at the other. On a good day, your machine runs smoothly and let's say, for argument's sake, for every 100 leads fed in twenty-five satisfied customers emerge. A 25% conversion rate is healthy, right? Everyone goes home happy.
>
> If you're working in a business where one in four leads turns into revenue, you might set yourself the task of chasing more leads. Why not? Two hundred would lead to fifty customers and you've doubled your money. This thinking, however, forgets the levers, pulleys, cogs and chutes that make up your business. No factory would double capacity without planning. Martin's focus on numbers encouraged me to apply an engineer's analytical eye to GoLocalise. Knowing how many leads we could realistically manage, at any given time, avoided wasting time and effort chasing contracts we didn't have the capacity to fulfil.
>
> This proved vital during the pandemic. Any kind of forecasting, of course, became a challenging activity. At times, frankly, we knew we didn't have enough

> work. Fortunately, we were able to reshuffle and readjust the cogs and levers to help the business pull through. We created hybrid roles, took advantage of the furlough scheme and adapted the best we could. All the while, Martin was on hand to provide me with coaching support, lend me a friendly ear and hold me accountable for decisions and results. As well as this, and countless other useful insights, I owe Martin a lot for introducing me to the work of Daniel Priestley – the next on the list of bulletproof people.

Daniel Priestley: The inspirational author who showed me what my business was worth

Daniel Priestley has another big brain that I, and many others, have learned a lot from. His book, *24 Assets: Create a digital, scalable, valuable and fun business that will thrive in a fast changing world*,[11] shares what it takes to become a successful business owner without sugar-coating the process. He doesn't share tales of entrepreneurs getting lucky, hiring the right people, creating cool products and taking off to earn millions. He has no shortcuts when it comes to fast growth, huge numbers and early retirement. He knows, in reality, most businesses require hard work, sacrifice and struggle, and that there are no guarantees of creating lasting value let alone spectacular riches. I was immediately drawn to this grounded world view. It felt real to me; then, in a moment of synchronicity,

---

11 Priestley, D, *24 Assets: Create a digital, scalable, valuable and fun business that will thrive in a fast changing world* (Rethink Press, 2017)

having heard of Daniel's theories through Martin, I got to meet him. He came to our GoLocalise studios to record the audio version of his book.

WORDS: Translation interlude

Have you played the Six Degrees of Kevin Bacon game? It is much beloved by Hollywood movie fans and illustrates the concept that, whether we like it or not, we're all unconsciously interconnected through our work. The game is based on the notion that, as a professional and hardworking actor, Kevin Bacon has worked with every star you can imagine. As a result, the Six Degrees of Kevin Bacon game asks participants to find films that link the star to others. Can you link Kevin Bacon to Emma Thompson, for example? The answer is yes – in two steps. Kevin Bacon was in *JFK* with Vincent D'Onofrio, who was in a documentary called *Lennon or McCartney* with the British actor. The theory goes that you can link Kevin Bacon to any other actor in this way and it will never take more than six steps.

This idea of interconnectedness, as we often find when we study the etymology of language, is far older than we initially might imagine. It was first proposed in 1929 by a Hungarian writer called Frigyes Karinthy.[12] He claimed, long before we had big-budget movie cast lists to compare, that any person could be connected to any other person in a chain of five intermediaries. This was explored further in the Pulitzer Prize-winning play called *Six Degrees of Separation*[13] by American

---

12 Karinthy, F, *Chains* (publisher unknown, 1929), http://vadeker.net/articles/Karinthy-Chain-Links_1929.pdf, accessed 31 March 2023
13 Guare, J. *Six Degrees of Separation* (Methuen Drama, 2010)

> playwright John Guare, from which the Kevin Bacon game lifts its title. In Hungarian, the six degrees of relationship theory translates as *hat fokos kapcsolat elmélet*. In Swedish it is *sex graders Förhållande teori*, in Kurdish it is *Têkiliya şeş derece dîtinî* and in Vietnamese it is *Quan hệ sáu độ học thuyết*. There is something sobering in the theory that we are closer to each other than we think. In business, I have had countless experiences, like my relationships with Martin and Daniel, that prove we are all operating in an increasingly small world. Or, as the Spanish would say, 'The world is a handkerchief' (*El mundo es un pañuelo*).

Hearing Daniel read his book, his passion for his subject became clear. He is committed to helping businesses create real value. Real value, I've come to realise, means having assets that one could sell when the time comes. It seems obvious when you sit and think about it, but it took Daniel's work for me to realise hard work is not automatically translated into tangible benefits or, indeed, a secure future. My interpretation of Daniel's thinking in *24 Assets*[14] is that any business needs a checklist to help plan for tomorrow. If, of the twenty-four assets he lists (including intellectual property, brand reputation, product features and innovative systems), I have twenty within GoLocalise, that makes for a good start. If it is just two or three, then I have work to do.

Through this logical and rational measure, Daniel's compelling arguments helped me understand the real

---

14 Priestley, D, *24 Assets: Create a digital, scalable, valuable and fun business that will thrive in a fast changing world* (Rethink Press, 2017)

value of my business. My perceived value, of course, based on all the sweat, blood and tears that I have put in is never going to be the same as an objective outsider's assessment, but it's a fair question. What would I do if I got the right offer from someone who wanted to buy GoLocalise and have me walk away?

At the point I picked Daniel's book up, I hadn't made any big decisions, but I was going through a time in my life when I was questioning GoLocalise's future, especially since I wanted to move to the USA to be with my partner. Daniel's invaluable book helped me prepare and identify areas of the business that needed attention and, in essence, made my future feel more secure – bulletproof even.

This chapter, and its lessons from when I started the business through to today, has been designed to encourage you to seek out and work with bulletproof people. I did this when I started the business, with Deborah, Javier and Roland, and later when things needed to change, with Martin and Daniel.

I know what it's like in the cut and thrust of running a business. It is easy to work with people out of convenience or because you are driven by cost. In the world of translators, for example, there is always someone who might be able to turn around work more quickly or at a lower rate. Taking shortcuts, however, especially when it comes to people, will often prove costly in the long run.

Whether you have been in business for years or are just starting out, my key lesson is to find the right collaborators. Suppliers, colleagues, gurus, coaches or advisors – call them what you will, but a team of bulletproof people around you will inevitably make you stronger. Even if, on occasion, they're not in a position to help directly, bulletproof contacts will, in the spirit of Kevin Bacon, be able to access their own networks to find good people who can. In this way, your list will grow in size and importance organically over time if you let it.

This might seem like an unsentimental, cold, professional view of working relationships. In all aspects of life, it is important to leave room for caring, sharing and genuine friendship. The list of bulletproof additions to the GoLocalise office team, for example, includes my dogs, Rocky and Rambo. Resolutely cheerful, always available for a hug and full of incredible energy, for many years they proved a huge support to me, my colleagues and even our clients, who made a point of saying hello and getting some love when they visited. Sadly, Rocky passed away in 2015, far too young, due to a heart murmur. He is desperately missed, but Rambo is still my bulletproof buddy.

> **WORDS: Translation interlude**
>
> To finish off this chapter, let's reflect on the value of finding people who understand you. We often take communication for granted, yet, despite our best efforts, there are still occasional moments when it fails

us and we face insurmountable problems. Some words and concepts remain enigmatically untranslatable, meaning we are sometimes genuinely lost for words. This is particularly true when we are asked to describe the highs and lows of the human condition.

The Czech word *litost* can't be contained in one word and can barely be explained in several English sentences. It has been described as a state of agony and torment created by the sudden sight of one's own misery. Words like this are more like moods in themselves: they describe conditions that people find themselves in as a direct result of a mountain of circumstances, and it seems almost to belittle the hardship that some people face to try and sum up their pain in six letters, but apparently this word does just that.

My advice would be to get bulletproof and avoid any chance of being *litost*, because it sounds awful.

On a brighter note, the Welsh word *cwtch* (one of many that do not have any vowels) is roughly translated as 'a safe place'. In reality, though, it describes the feeling of being safe that is transferred through the act of giving someone an affectionate hug, implying that certain people and their reassuring presence or touch can make you feel more secure. I think this ties in well with the idea of being bulletproof, because when I put one of my top people on a job I feel peace of mind. I am so happy to have such talented people surrounding my business that I often feel like hugging them.

The number of words with no direct translation into English is notably small. It is funny to think that the English language is pretty bulletproof in itself for no other reason than it has the most words to choose from. There are said to be over one million recorded English words,[15] and more than a dozen new ones are added each day. Some new additions to official English dictionaries in recent years include:

- Adulting: a verb that describes doing an activity associated with maturity such as paying taxes, buying property or investing in a pension scheme
- Doomscrolling: the problematic and addictive action of joylessly trawling through bad news on social media channels
- Whataboutism: a debate technique or practice, typical of identity politics, whereby an argument is countered with something unrelated to the original topic

---

15 GLM Admin, 'Number of words in the English language', The Global Language Monitor (16 December 2018), https://languagemonitor.com/number-of-words-in-english/no-of-words, accessed 31 March 2023

> - Staycation: a vacation spent in one's home country rather than abroad, or one spent at home and involving day trips to local attractions
> - Zooming: a redefined verb that doesn't mean you'll be moving quickly, but that you'll be chatting online

Like in all businesses, Zooming has become important to the team at GoLocalise. I also find it fascinating how quickly it became a new way of communicating – developing new practices and vocabulary seemingly overnight. How many times have we heard 'you're on mute' over the last three years? That said, I value face-to-face meetings a great deal and make sure to have them whenever time and geography allow it.

We've proved the English language is constantly on the move. It has more words than any other. It is one of the fastest growing and is spoken, as a major language, in more countries than any other. It is also the second most popular language around the globe measured by the number of people who speak it, after Mandarin Chinese. Yet, as we have seen throughout this book, it can still lack the appropriate words for every situation.

In some ways, that might suggest there are gaps in its armour or that it is not perfect, and there is a lesson here for people who want to stand out from the crowd and become bulletproof. Being bulletproof is not about being perfect; it is about being reliable and delivering a great result every time. It is about adapting to the situation, using all of your skills whether gained through natural ability, learned or practised. When this is combined with a diligent attitude to create something perfect (or as near to perfect as it is possible to be), it is powerful. Just like my other bulletproof friends, the English language is a great example of a tried-and-tested resource which is recognised as being a world leader but is also prepared to adapt and change.

That's certainly been the case in recent years. No matter how good you are, how great your reputation or how much experience you have, we have learned you can never stay still. There will always be things to learn. If arguably the most influential language on the planet has to keep adding new words (twelve to sixteen per day),[16] then even the most bulletproof of people should **be prepared to keep adapting** as well.

Surrounding myself with talented people I can trust is the best way I have come across to keep working at the top of my game and maintaining the quality of the work I deliver. It is a cliche to say 'you're only as good as your last job' but cliches become cliches because they are, ultimately, true. Let your network falter and your standards slide and you will start painfully letting the odd bullet through. Keep great people around you and you'll thrive.

---

16 GLM Admin, 'Number of words in the English language', The Global Language Monitor (16 December 2018), https://languagemonitor.com/number-of-words-in-english/no-of-words, accessed 31 March 2023

8
Translation That Others Could Understand

The first few years of running GoLocalise were a bit like going on a road trip without a destination. I was accelerating most of the time because I was determined to be a success. I was doing some of the right things, like actively looking for new customers and systemising my processes, but I didn't know where I was going or how to get off the back roads and onto the motorway. Looking back, I can see that effort gets results, but focused and well-directed effort gets far bigger results.

As the late great American entrepreneur, Jim Rohn, once said, 'If someone is going down the wrong road, he doesn't need motivation to speed him up. What he needs is education to turn him around.' I was in desperate need of education. I'd learned from some of the best in the industry, I knew how to put together a bulletproof translation, subtitle file or voice-over project, but I still needed help to run a business properly. I'd had a bad experience of working in partnership with someone, and I knew how painful it was to work in a company where the management hardly acknowledged the staff were alive. Conversely, I'd experienced the best of working environments and discovered that finding outstanding freelancers was worth the effort, but I had never successfully employed people.

My own efforts eventually took me to a place where I needed to translate what I believed and knew into a language potential employees could understand.

My accountant had advised me to set myself up as a limited company to benefit from some of the tax credits and allow me to get others involved, so GoLocalise Ltd was created in 2008. By 2010 I was earning a good wage personally and the business was growing steadily. My customers were happy, I had built a solid network of voice-over and translation talent, and on the face of it there didn't seem to be a problem. There was a problem. In fact, there were two problems going on behind the scenes. Firstly, the long working days were taking their toll. Being the only employee in my business meant that I was responsible for everything that happened within it and had to give it twelve to sixteen hours a day, and that level of effort, concentration and responsibility simply is not sustainable. Interestingly, when you are in the midst of a lifestyle like that you hardly notice the hours, but when you finally manage to escape it, you can see the dangers and the damage that you might have done to yourself.

The other problem was related to the first. Because I was operating at my capacity, and at times was on the verge of collapsing, there was nowhere else for the business to go. My mum often says, 'If you don't let water flow, it will become stale', meaning that life is like a river which needs to keep moving forward. This is true in many things (thanks, Mum), and I've learned that nowhere is it more relevant than in business, so I knew then that I had to get other people involved in GoLocalise. If I didn't, the whole thing was going to fail before it had got properly started.

In 2010 I decided (or rather, my circumstances forced me) to let the water flow. I got lucky with my first full-time employee, Martina, who initially joined as a sound engineer but then got involved in some project management work. Having an employee was a revelation to me. I lost some of my personal income, yes, but I gained the time to re-engage with my personal goals. Shortly after Martina joined, I suddenly remembered why I had gone into the business in the first place.

In that instant, clarity descended in my head and my business vision became crystal clear: I was going to create a great working environment. I would surround myself with people who believed in the same things as me, and then I would grow my business. Soon I'd employed more people to take up the practical and technical roles within the business, keeping the good ones and letting the others go. They were primarily sound engineers and project managers, but often their roles involved multitasking and getting involved wherever there was a need. It was working, and eventually we needed to move to a bigger office.

We had been operating out of an apartment on Warren Street which I had lived in for eight years then turned into an office just about adequate for my growing team, but when the landlord decided to sell the property it seemed an appropriate time to move on. With a two-month window, I set about finding a building that would house my ambitious expansion plans.

I found a place in Stockwell fairly quickly which ticked most of the boxes in that it was close to the Tube, within my budget and the right size, but it was far from perfect at the time. I was clear in my mind what I wanted: an attractive office space, two recording studios, stylish decor – a place where people could work happily, which meant going back to long days for a while and having more than a few battles with the builders, insisting that they stick to my plans. We got there with only a few hours left of the two-month deadline, and once again the chorizo sandwiches came out in celebration.

I remember the moving day well (and the date even better). On 11/11/11 GoLocalise moved into its current office in Stockwell.

LESSON: Deadlines and time-integrity get stuff done

The move into our offices within the deadline is a great analogy for getting important things done in business. Often people identify something as being a good thing to do, either in life or business, but they never get around to doing it. As one of my most important business mentors, Nigel Botterill (more about Nigel later), says, 'Most people are world-class at getting ready', meaning that few people ever press 'go'. On this occasion, the move was forced upon us, along with the deadline, and because we had to make a big and complex project happen accurately and on time, we succeeded. The thing to learn from this is that you can create your own deadlines and goals, and that is powerful.

Imagine the same scenario, the only difference being that I had decided to move. Rather than having to be out of the old premises on 11/11/11, I had decided that date was my target. If I showed the same integrity to my own goals that I had shown to necessity, I would achieve the same result. In practice, however, I would have had the option to prolong and procrastinate. Would I have done? Who knows?

I try to apply this lesson to everything that we do in the business today. Whether it is a project for a customer, a change in the process or a marketing campaign, we set a reasonable finish time and, as a team, take responsibility for the goal. It sounds simple, but setting and keeping deadlines has been one of the most important principles in the growth of my business, and we rarely let ourselves off the hook. This is another lesson that I learned from Nigel Botterill.

We settled into the building quickly, largely because everything was already in place to hit the ground running, and embarked on the next stage of growth. Part of my plan and vision, especially with the new facilities and space available, was to make the business bulletproof and then focus on a big push for new customers.

That meant two things had to happen. Firstly, I needed to learn about sales and marketing properly, as I realised that spamming probably wasn't going to work this time. Secondly, I needed to systemise all of the processes that my staff were doing manually, which would increase both the efficiency and accuracy of everything we did. That was when I started getting the FileMaker system together. For now, let me share the woes of employing sales staff who don't know how to sell.

I started off by employing a marketing expert, or so it said on his CV, but he turned out to be a designer (I would even say he was quite a good designer) and, to my detriment, I soon learned that there is a difference. I liked him as a person, but he wasn't the person I needed in my business.

I agreed to pay him a salary, and from day one explained that I needed him to get me more customers in return, but for just under twelve months all I got was some shelf-filling brochures and Internet content. It wasn't the result I was looking for. What I needed was a way to identify people who used services like ours and attract their attention. I then needed to work out exactly what they were looking for and create a message which showed them how we could fulfil that need in their lives. Once we'd created that brief and devised a strategy to fulfil it, then it might have been a good idea to get some marketing collateral together, but I know now that my marketing 'expert' didn't know that then. It all ended up being an expensive disaster, made even worse by the fact that I had to get rid of a nice person.

Looking back, I can see that I employed someone without fully knowing what I needed, but it still caused me nearly twelve months of expense-draining pain with little gain. Even worse was that I then went and made another similarly expensive mistake straight away when I employed a salesperson.

At the beginning of 2013 I took on the person who was going to get me all the customers I would ever need. It was obvious – need sales? Get a salesperson. Wrong. I was still missing the point – I knew my customers and understood the value that they saw in us, but I had fallen into the trap of trying to find a magic pill to fix a problem rather than working out what the problem was first.

As is the way with most 'great ideas', everything started off well and offered great promise. My new salesperson arrived on her first day. She was charming, everyone liked her and she enthusiastically set about learning the business and finding me new customers. It was only later that I worked out why she had been a top performer in her previous role. She had worked for a large hotel chain where her role revolved around building relationships with an existing customer base, not finding new ones. Any new business that had come her way was the result of her answering the phone; she rarely made outgoing calls, and certainly never to sell.

Once again, I realise that ultimately I have to take responsibility for whom I employ. The crunch came one quiet afternoon early in 2014. After several salesless months, we had a meeting where I encouraged her to make some calls and try to generate meetings, and it was then that she explained how different the role was to what she had been used to and had expected. She then said that she didn't feel comfortable making calls. I responded by suggesting that I didn't feel comfortable paying a salesperson not to sell.

Soon afterwards she left the company. It might sound a little cruel to say that no one noticed, but when you run a small business the areas that aren't bulletproof are noticeable. No longer having to pay her salary was certainly the biggest contribution she had made for some time.

> **LESSON: You are in charge of your decisions, so take responsibility for them**
>
> While I am a little embarrassed to this day to admit I made two similar mistakes in a row, I had finally learned my lesson and there was no way I was going

> to go there again. From that time onwards, I took it upon myself to learn everything I could about sales and marketing, just as I had learned to be a sound technician, worked as a voice-over artist, managed large translation projects and run the back-office processes before employing help.
>
> What I have learned in my business, and from every successful business owner I know, is that the more you know about a role, the better you can manage someone else doing it. Nigel Botterill states, 'No one will ever care about your business as much as you do', and I have found that to be true.
>
> To grow your business effectively, you need to employ brilliant (bulletproof) people. To manage those people well, you have two basic choices: employ managers you trust (meaning that you are certain of their heart and ability) to deliver the results you need, or learn at least the basics of the role you are asking your employee to do. If you don't know what 'doing it well' looks like, then how are you ever going to measure success?

I set myself a task of studying marketing and observing other people who seemed to be getting it right. In the next chapter, I will share the most exciting part of my journey to date and the lessons that changed my destiny.

9
A New World Of Ideas And Opportunity

Ironically, during my two years of sales and marketing fiascos, the business had been growing organically, but this did not disguise the lack of results. I knew our existing customers were giving us lots of additional work, and the more these accounts grew, the more vulnerable I felt. While I was confident that the great service we delivered and the strong relationships we had built meant the business was secure with these clients, it still felt a little uncomfortable. I recognised that we were highly dependent on a few large accounts, and for that reason I wanted to get new customers.

Then the worst-case scenario actually happened. Around the beginning of 2014 our largest client lost one of their key contracts, and the knock-on effect meant nearly 50% of our turnover disappeared overnight. I had been through two years of stress and woe, so what do you think that did for my good night's sleep? I was devastated, and more than a little bit afraid for the business and my staff. It seemed like a volley of bullets had been launched at us, and as most of them had got through I felt far from bullet-proof that day, I can tell you. Despite all of my efforts to create a successful business, modelled on what I'd learned from my experiences up to that point, it seemed that circumstance was going to be a party pooper and ruin the day.

WORDS: Translation interlude

Imagine the fun that translators have had with the expression 'party pooper' over the years. It brings up images that are far from pleasant, but in reality it comes from the 1950s when the term 'pooped out' meant exhausted. The phrase, therefore, represents people who bring down the tone or life of a party by

> their actions, or by leaving it altogether. In my case it felt like circumstances were threatening to suck the life out of the business I'd worked so hard to build, but I was not going to let that happen. I realised I had made a mistake that I could rectify by not putting all my eggs into one basket in the future.
>
> Interestingly, the phrase 'don't put all your eggs in one basket' is one which doesn't need much explanation in any language, as far as I know. It is totally self-evident, especially in relation to stories such as mine.

I was determined not to lose any of my staff for two reasons. Firstly, I liked them, and I knew that this particular situation was not their fault or in any way a reflection on their work. Secondly, and perhaps more commercially, they had proved themselves to be great assets to my business. Their record made me confident that, going forward, I would be better off with them than without them. They were important to me on many levels.

This just added rocket fuel to my determination to make the business work, so I took out an £80k personal loan and gave it to the company to cover wages and running costs in the months that followed. Big pressure, but often it is from places like these in your life that you make the biggest decisions and see them through. My promise to myself was **never again**, so I set about learning sales and marketing. I read as much as I could, talked to all the salespeople I knew, studied and stalked those who were successful in my marketplace, and others. I signed up for AdWords courses, Facebook courses and marketing courses, and I finally stumbled over the answer.

> **LESSON: When faced with sink or swim, choose to swim with everything you've got**
>
> Sometimes in business you have to hold your breath for a while, and there are two ways to do this. Either you work out how long you can go underwater (or into debt) and then create a plan which will get you back to the surface quickly enough, or you hold your breath for as long as you possibly can, hoping against hope that you find some sort of air supply or escape before your lungs burst. I have always been a bit reckless and perhaps there was an element of the second scenario involved in my decision, but I certainly believed that my heart was big enough to get out quickly enough, whatever happened.
>
> The lesson here is that if you identify a problem which will eventually drown you, you are only prolonging the inevitable by waiting. The expression 'sink or swim' means there are two options. My experience, and I'm sure that universal truth would agree, is that those who stand and fight have a far better chance of winning than those who cower away and give up. There is another important thing to remember when faced with an all-or-nothing situation – make sure you fight wisely, not just with a big heart and your lungs full of belief-fuelled air.

Fairly soon after I had decided to take out the loan and learn about sales and marketing for myself, I saw a Facebook post from a voice-over artist I knew well and had worked with before. Rachael Naylor was celebrated and well known in the industry, and she posted that she had just won the Entrepreneur of the Month Award at the Entrepreneurs Circle. It wasn't the first time I had heard of this organisation, but as they were one of many that had marketed to me (they obviously knew something about prospect behaviours), I hadn't responded to them. After speaking to Rachael and getting a glowing report, I got in touch with the Entrepreneurs Circle and signed up. In fact, I was so impressed with the feedback from Rachael and the person who'd answered the phone at the Entrepreneurs Circle (Frahana) that I jumped in with both feet. The organisation had an entry-level trial offer on at the time, but I figured as I was already underwater, why not swim deeper? My experience told me that all or nothing drives the best results, and I later discovered that this is a typical character trait of successful entrepreneurs, so I was in good company.

I went in at club-level membership from day one because I knew that only 100% commitment would get 100% results, and it worked. Suddenly I had access to a whole team of people who wanted to help me, teach me and provoke me into getting the customers I needed to make my business work again. I'd been swimming around underwater when suddenly a blue-and-red submarine appeared and I was invited inside. Don't get me wrong, I was still responsible for doing the work, but from that point on I did it with shared wisdom, direction, support and encouragement.

It reminded me a little bit of my childhood. I'd been through a tough time, felt alone and frightened, and then my family had stepped in and sent me off to further my education. Back then it had been to keep me busy and out of trouble; this time, it was to keep me in business and able to outpace trouble. I found solace, direction and a new lease of life in this world of entrepreneurial success, and finally I was able to breathe freely again.

The thing with family is that you learn to trust them. A bond starts in your early months and it quickly becomes unbreakable, especially if you receive the things necessary for you to grow. I took hold of everything that was offered to me by the Entrepreneurs Circle and the change in my business was remarkable. As I learned to trust what I was taught, I grew closer to the Entrepreneurs Circle family, and within five months I'd joined one of their Mastermind Groups. This came with a significant five-figure cost for the year, but by this time, I no longer saw the investment as going underwater. Rather, I was buying a speedboat to get across the surface faster. Guess what – that worked too.

Having lost 50% of my turnover the previous year, the following twelve months saw it grow by 400%. I would put that growth almost entirely down to sound business education and implementation. Hard work too, of course.

WORDS: Translation interlude

Talking of business mishaps, here are a few more stories which didn't quite translate into global successes:

- When Ford decided to use a successful US campaign in the European market, it gave a different impression to what they had intended. Being proud of its Detroit heritage and the quality of its world-class manufacturing, Ford ran with the slogan 'Every car has a high-quality body'. This had worked well in the USA, fitting in with what people already knew of Detroit's car-manufacturing history and believed of Ford, but people in Holland feared more of a Chicago or New York Mafia connection as the phrase translated into 'Every car has a high-quality corpse'. It was not an appealing proposal, and more than a few boots ('trunks' in the USA) were checked at the point of sale.

- Sometimes it is not the words which are the problem, because translation covers far more than just verbal communication. One such case was when Proctor and Gamble launched their Pampers nappies range in Japan. As in other countries where they had won a large market share, they used their familiar image of a stork carrying a baby, but being a story which had been born out of Greek and Roman mythology and later popularised in German then European folklore, the idea of storks bringing babies into the world was alien to the Japanese. When they finally worked out what the problem was, the company changed the packaging – that was one campaign which didn't have wings.

- What do you do when it is your company name causing the translation difficulty? Another American company, Gerber, is a large producer of baby food with a recognised brand all over the USA. Currently, the company focuses all of its marketing and sales efforts on its home market, and that might be down to a particular incident while promoting its products in French-speaking Canada. In French, the word *gerber* means 'to vomit' – not a particularly attractive idea considering the target market, and one that threw up a few problems for the marketing department.

The Entrepreneurs Circle is headed by Nigel Botterill, whom I've mentioned a few times before, and it was one of Nigel's personal Mastermind Groups that I joined at the end of 2014. It would take a whole book to translate all the things I have learned from him into lessons to share with you, but I have to say that his impact on me has been massive. It was he who inspired my award-winning streak.

That leads me nicely on to one of my proudest moments. Please bear with my self-indulgence, not just because I enjoyed the achievement, but because I am keen to get across that you can reach the targets you aim for if you combine effort and desire. It is also a nice way to bring the story of my sales and marketing adventure full circle.

I mentioned that it was seeing Rachael's Entrepreneur of the Month Award that drew my attention to the Entrepreneurs Circle in the first place. Well, in May 2015 I was recognised for the same achievement, based on the growth of my business as well as all the marketing implementation I had been doing. From there I got the bug for recognition and decided to create an award strategy. Over the next few months I entered other business competitions and submitted the things GoLocalise had been doing as evidence of our achievements. The feedback was remarkable and, before we knew it, the awards started flowing in. We won Outstanding Business in the Global Business Excellence Awards, Best Product/Service Range in the Best Business Awards, and the Outstanding Entrepreneur categories in both sets of awards. At the time of the first edition of this book going to print, early in 2016, a few more awards had been added to the shelf (and I hope there will be many more to follow). These were personal awards, also associated with the Entrepreneurs Circle, that I am proud of – at the end of 2015 I was voted Most Inspiring Member for the South East Region of the Circle, and I was a finalist in the big one: the Entrepreneur of the Year.

LESSON: What is an entrepreneur anyway?

The word 'entrepreneur' is borrowed from French and was first used in the 1700s. Its literal meaning describes someone who undertakes a task or venture, but today it has far more dynamic, even romantic, connotations, and embodies the spirit of adventure in those who set off into unknown territories to start up new businesses. It implies innovation, leadership, courage, business intelligence and passion for learning, growing and sharing.

In my experience, there are business owners and there are entrepreneurs, in the same way that there are those who are good at what they do and those who love it. To run a business, you need to be able to make the numbers add up, employ capable people and keep the boat afloat. To be an entrepreneur means that you cannot resist a challenge, an idea, the lure of an opportunity or the chance to get involved in something new. It is a wonderful occupation, but it comes with more than its fair share of pitfalls to negotiate. I don't think that anyone chooses to be an entrepreneur; it is a vocation which calls you, gets under your skin and won't let go until you reach for your dreams. You do have choices within this calling, though, and I would urge any would-be entrepreneur to take one of these choices seriously.

Entrepreneurship can be a lonely path to walk, but it doesn't have to be. You do not have to walk it alone. In fact, you will be far better off if you don't, but who you choose to hold your hand matters – a lot. I hardly need to repeat the qualities I would look for in a business partner (whether formally or informally); suffice to say that being bulletproof would be near the top of the list.

That is how my business got through its toughest challenges to date, and how I discovered the way to turn it into something more enterprising.

In the next chapter, I am going to introduce you to a few more people who have made an impact in my life and business. I will explore the power of recognising potential, the value in appreciating the help that others give you, and the amazing feeling of being able to give something back.

PART FOUR
THE BIG LESSON AND THE WAY FORWARD

10
Making Friends Makes Good Business Sense

Some of the best things in life are not easy to recognise at first glance, and sometimes that means you need to pursue them or use a little imagination to bring them to light. I want to illustrate this by telling you how I met my good friend Patricia Rodríguez.

Let me take you back to my childhood. Many years ago, back home in Gijón, Ita (my grandma) worked as a nurse at the local hospital, and one of her colleagues had a daughter called Patricia. Although we grew up in the same town and my parents and grandparents were good friends with her parents, we'd never formally met, but as is the custom in small Spanish towns, any acquaintance of the family is as good as a long-lost cousin, especially when you're living in foreign lands.

Back in 2009 I was about to board the plane from Asturias Airport back to England after a trip home. I was waiting to go through customs when my mum and Ita started speaking excitedly to a lady who turned out to be Patricia's mum. Coincidently, Patricia had just gone through the gate, and because she was also living in London, they decided that we were destined to become best friends forever. I was given clear instructions on how to recognise her when I went through – she was wearing a purple pullover, had curly hair and would be reading a book. What could be simpler?

Now I don't know if you remember the winter of 2009, so let me jog your memory. Purple was suddenly 'in', as was curly hair, maybe because *Harry Potter and the Half-Blood Prince* had just been released, or maybe it was a case of the Baader-Meinhof phenomenon.[17] Whatever the reason, there must have been twenty purple-topped girls with varying degrees of curly hair sitting in the waiting area, reading books. I am not a particularly shy person, but the idea of systematically asking each of them their name, address and phone number didn't seem right somehow, so that is how I almost met someone who had been born in the same town as me and whose family had been good friends with mine for decades.

All was not lost, though, because the other thing people from small Spanish towns like to do is follow up

---

17 Nikolopoulou, K, 'The Baader-Meinhof phenomenon explained', Scribbr (2 November 2022, revised 18 November 2022), www.scribbr.co.uk/bias-in-research/baader-meinhof, accessed 31 March 2023

to make sure introductions are carried out. A few days after I got home, Patricia called me and we arranged to meet up. I specifically requested that she didn't wear purple.

As it turned out, she was an actor who ran a fabulous independent theatre production company called Little Soldier Productions. She was looking for extra work, and I'm always keen to find good new voice-over talent, so she recorded a demo and we started working on a few projects together. I have since had the great honour of supporting some of her stunning theatre productions, we've conducted interviews together, helped arrange theatre tours and even produced trailers for shows. It is great to be friends and work with such a talented person.

> LESSON: Recognising talent and perfect customers is paramount
>
> Being able to recognise people is important in business. There is an old saying (presumably a generic business one rather than a language-specific one) which states that it is not what you know, but who you know. This is relevant whether you are looking for staff and business partners to help you grow, or for suppliers to support the work you are doing. When I say 'support', I mean in terms of matching your values, standards and quality commitment, not just by doing some work – so it does help if you know or know of somebody before you start looking. That way you have already got an insight into their character, history or style.

Sometimes, however, you have to start looking from scratch. You don't know anyone who fits the space you need to fill, so your only option is to put out an advert or spread the word that you are looking. There is a powerful weapon that you can bring into play, and it involves a purple pullover.

Whenever you are looking for new staff, new freelancers, a new job, or anything in life where you have no inside information or contacts to help you out, simply create the perfect image in your mind or on a piece of paper. Decide what that person should be like, how they should act, what drives and motivates them, and even what they might be doing now, then go and look for that specific (if imaginary) person.

There must have been hundreds, maybe thousands of people in the airport lounge that day. They would have been shopping, drinking coffee, daydreaming about England or reading a book. If my life or livelihood had depended on finding Patricia, the good friend I didn't even know I had, it would have been easy simply because I knew enough about her. As it turned out, it wasn't what I knew, it was who I knew which helped me out on that occasion, but with a little effort I could have done it on my own.

A final thought on this, but a massively important one: you can identify, find and convert new customers in this way as well. All you need to do is decide what your perfect customer looks like (wearing purple, curly hair, head in a book, etc) and then start asking questions that will attract their attention.

Most businesses start by thinking about what they want to sell rather than who might like to buy it. This is a massive mistake and is why many new companies

> stay small or fail altogether. If the majority of people in your marketplace are crying out to buy purple pullovers, there is no point in making orange ones just because that is your expertise or preference. You must know what your potential customers want, but to be the most successful you have to go even further than simply knowing what they want. You need to make sure that the market knows you too, so wearing a purple pullover yourself and telling wonderful stories about the colour purple would be a great idea.

I recognised long ago (it probably goes right back to the values I was taught as a child) that giving something back is important. As I got into business and learned about the value of building relationships, it became apparent to me that I could combine a little philanthropy with my work. What didn't occur to me, until I saw it come to fruition, was just how valuable that practice would be for the business, and the more selfless the giving, the better the return seemed to be.

Since 2011 GoLocalise has been running Christmas parties to raise money for charities like Great Ormond Street Hospital and Action for Children. Of course, being the host of the event, and the communications expert, it was down to me to mispronounce the name of the charity each time I stepped up to the microphone. At the time, I was unsure why my audience laughed at me whenever I said 'Children in Action' as though I was encouraging a re-opening of the workhouse society.

The other area where I have enjoyed being able to share my experiences is speaking to linguistics students at UCL and other universities. This is something that I want to continue doing in the future as I am grateful to the people who have influenced my journey up to this point. It is wonderful to be able to share the things I have seen, learned and experienced with young people who echo my passion for language. You see, like everything else in life, simply being passionate about something is rarely going to supply people with all the ammunition they need to be successful at it. They need to learn the system, the rules of the game, the way that the marketplace works, the way that other people behave, and how to manage the problems that will arise. I talk to the students about all of these things, and teach them about being bulletproof.

It is a given that you will face tough times, whether through your own failings, circumstances you can't control or someone else letting you down, so the thing I talk about more than anything else when I go into universities is how to become bulletproof. I want the students to realise that life will let them down, but if they can take a volley of bullets aimed at them, they can always carry on.

Before I leave this chapter on friends and influences, I need to introduce you to one more person who has helped me immensely, both early on and to this day.

My former manager at Technicolor was Stewart Dickison, and it was his direction as much as working for the company itself which made it such a great experience. He taught me a lot about the translation market, from doing the work through to dealing with people and creating processes that would later become essential to my own business. Ironically, the most important lesson he taught me came on the day he made me redundant.

It was clear that he took the situation forced upon him personally. He had created a great environment for us to work in and, in return, we had worked hard for him and gone the extra mile wherever needed, so when it came to closing down that happy chapter in all of our lives, he was probably the saddest of all. He did it with understanding and dignity, offered his support to help us get new jobs, wrote sparkling recommendation letters to help us on our way, and kept in touch. Those of us who did made a friend for life, even though we went to work for rival companies after that.

LESSON: Building bridges and burning them

In business, there are times when you need to make a clean break and move on. It can be a tough environment, and there is little mercy shown when it comes to personal ambition. People are suspicious of each other, office politics is rife and the jostling for position when promotions are up for grabs can be an unpleasant sight; but when you find genuine people in business, as in life, they are the ones who are worth working for and with. When you make genuine friendships, treasure them.

It is well known that people show their true colours in a crisis, and those who remain true at those times are worth their weight in gold or, as the English expression goes, 'a friend in need is a friend indeed'. This is another element of being bulletproof for me. Being reliable as a supplier, an employee, a manager and a friend are the things people will remember you for the most, and I have learned that it is possible to be strong in business, be ruthless when it is absolutely necessary, and still do the right thing and be a good, reliable person.

Tough times will come, but there is no value in burning bridges just because an unavoidable problem caused something to go wrong. The solid bridges we build in life will give us a place to find support, find answers and move on. Likewise, maintaining these bridges is how we help our friends in return when they need it. Familiar things like family, life-long friendships, trusted colleagues, bulletproof people and chorizo sandwiches can make all the difference.

To finish this chapter, I want to leave you with some more of my favourite words that do not exist outside of their language of origin.

WORDS: Translation interlude

The word *Ilunga* is a Congolese personal name, which is also used as a word in the Tshiluba language of south-eastern Democratic Republic of the Congo. It was once voted in a survey of 1,000 linguists as being the world's most untranslatable word. Roughly, it means 'a person who is ready to forgive any abuse the first time, tolerate it a second time, but never a third time'.

I love this idea because it is relevant to my experiences in business. Being the best you can is important, but it is also good practice to give people the benefit of the doubt sometimes. Whether you keep doing that indefinitely or not, though, is the difference between being a good person and a pushover.

In Russia, there is a word for someone who asks too many questions. The word is *pochemuchka*, derived from the Russian for 'why', and it was popularised by a children's book about a child who was overcurious about everything. For me, being *pochemuchka* is a

> good thing, and I would encourage it in anyone who wants to get better at whatever they do in life.
>
> The word 'bulletproof' itself is a relatively new addition to all languages, because before the invention of bullets around the 1500s there wasn't any need for it. The idea would have existed long before then, however, in the words 'invincible', 'invulnerable' or by being reliable, and the same thing applies in the business world. The basic concepts of business have existed in various formats since humankind started to trade. Today we just deal with business through different media: the Internet, the telephone, rapid transport and global trading. We have invented new ways to deal with old problems, but as with being bulletproof, the basic idea remains the same: become good at what you do, deliver great results consistently and learn to get on well with other people.

In the final chapter, I will sum up all of the things that my story has taught me about living in a different country. It is my final word on becoming bulletproof.

11
Getting Older And Wiser And Running A More Mature Business

A sign things had started to change in my life was a growing interest from others in buying GoLocalise from me. 'Is it for sale?' people would ask. 'What are your plans for the future?' 'Do you want a way out?' 'Can they help with my exit strategy?' The questions sometimes came from contacts resurfacing from my past. Other times, it was strangers reaching out by email or through LinkedIn. They varied in tone from gentle enquiries that went around the houses to more direct, aggressive offers that cut to the chase. They were typically from representatives of much bigger businesses who, I guessed, thought it would be a good move to acquire an existing audiovisual department (translation and subtitling agency and voice-over studio) to expand their business service portfolio.

This, to me, clearly marked the fact I had crossed a particular line in the sand. I had moved from being a young newcomer on the block to the owner of a mature, established company. Purchasing GoLocalise had become a sensible, reasonable alternative to starting an equivalent business from scratch. This felt like a moment to celebrate, even if I wasn't actively considering selling. I did have a few conversations with several of these potential buyers, but discussions never proceeded far. The thing that didn't work, always, was the fact we couldn't agree on the value. I knew what all the heartache, blood, sweat and tears I had contributed to GoLocalise was worth to me and, you guessed it, their offers were always way too low. I couldn't, however, easily put my finger on the right price. If I'm being honest with myself, any figure I came up with was significantly inflated by emotion. To move forward, I needed to think with my head not my heart and understand my business's value rationally and objectively.

Wondering about my business's value in this way didn't mean I had immediate plans to sell it. I still don't, but I will one day. What will GoLocalise need to be sales-ready? This was the real question I found myself needing an answer to. Unless you have skipped ahead, you'll already have read about the people who helped me with this dilemma in Chapter 7. Specifically, I describe the book *24 Assets*[18] by the excellent

---

18 Priestley, D, *24 Assets: Create a digital, scalable, valuable and fun business that will thrive in a fast changing world* (Rethink Press, 2017)

Daniel Priestley and share how it helped me with this precise challenge.

I immediately found his way of viewing business useful. Like an old-school fan, I hung on to his every word and even asked him to sign a copy of the book for me. I still treasure it and refer to it from time to time as I make business decisions. His lessons around value and growth landed at just the right time for me. By late 2019 I was planning a change to my lifestyle with a new husband, and my business was attracting interest from potential purchasers. There couldn't have been a better time to consider a realistic view of GoLocalise's value and what that might mean to my future.

I still enjoyed running the business and I felt I would for the foreseeable future. I have still, as I write this, quickly turned down anyone interested in purchasing the business. I have always politely, but firmly, asked for a potential purchase price and, so far, it has never been right for me, and I go back to work.

A key word here is 'realistic', of course. We all dream of the billion-dollar status of Facebook, Twitter, Google and the like but the fact that such Silicon Valley stories are referred to as 'unicorns' tells the tale. They are one-in-a-million, if not one-in-a-billion, successes that owe their existence to numerous technological and social strands colliding at just the right moment. I suspect consciously chasing similar success would drive you to distraction. Realistic, for me, means balancing the needs of any purchaser with my exit plans. If we can agree on a fair price when the time comes, I will be happy.

Even if any sale feels years away, having a greater understanding of GoLocalise's value lets me plan for the next ten, twenty or even thirty years. Do I want enough in the bank when I say goodbye to fund a retirement of endless luxury travel and nonstop partying? If that turns out to be the plan, I may need to up my game to get the right price to pay for it all. Even a more modest ambition, such as caring for myself and my family in old age, needs careful planning.

Part of being an older and wiser business owner, compared to being a young thrusting entrepreneur, is the fact you can see an end in sight. Thanks to interest from potential buyers and the work of Daniel Priestley, I was in a more measured frame of mind and able to plan the next big step in my life. At least for a while… Now I need to issue a spoiler warning because everything was about to change.

> **LESSON: Get your business sales-ready**
>
> As we've established, considering your exit as a business owner does not necessarily mean you have imminent plans to sell. Thinking of future potential purchasers down the line is a useful way to work out the things your business is doing well and the areas that need

> improvement. For example, by asking yourself if your business is ready to sell, you might identify the fact that you have a popular and attractive product. You might also realise, however, that you have an inefficient costly manufacturing process which is not. Your brand reputation might have value, but this will be limited if it is based solely on people likely to leave under new management. This may even be you if you play a high-profile role in your business. It's hard to see lasting value in business if the core skills and capabilities that make it special are solely based on employees. In a sales-ready business, value comes from the unique way things are done, rather than who does them.

I soon realised the success of GoLocalise, moving forward, needed to depend less on my direct management input and more on the machine that I created with my team. When a business is mature and sales-ready, the owner's role can switch from operational day-to-day management to strategy and planning for the future. My role has moved in this direction over the last two to three years because of the work I have done to ensure our machine runs smoothly and our bulletproof quality of service remains uninterrupted.

It can be hard work getting there, but it's a great feeling knowing your business operates effectively without you needing to worry about every last detail. I spent the time putting systems and processes in place to get us there only because I started to consider GoLocalise's future value. Even if I do not sell for decades, it has been a useful exercise.

WORDS: Translation interlude

Business efficiency, on the face of it, might seem a dull, dry and dusty subject. Perhaps one for the mathematicians rather than the linguists? Nonsense. Language, as we know, has a habit of adding colour to any subject by borrowing from history. In English, things 'can go without a hitch' or 'run like clockwork'. The 'i's can be dotted and the t's crossed' and everything can be 'ship-shape', 'A-OK' and 'tickety boo'. Tickety boo sounds particularly delightful to me. It is thought to be the Hindi phrase '*thik hai, babu*' ('it's alright, Sir') adapted and imported by the English aristocracy from the days of the Indian Raj. There are, of course, local idioms that say the same thing in every language. A process might be '*bułka z masłem*', 'a roll with butter', in Polish, for example, which equates to 'a piece of cake'. An Italian might describe a job that was easy as an '*un gioco da bambini*', meaning, literally, 'a children's game'.

Imagine hearing your business described in these ways. It feels good, doesn't it? The alternative? Less so. You wouldn't want to hear a Russian customer exclaim блин (*blin*) when working with your team. Translated as 'pancake' or 'flapjack', it is an expletive born of frustration that you might hear muttered through gritted teeth. If things aren't alright, a Hindi customer might call you the 'son of an owl' (*Ullu ka Patta*) because, unlike the wise old birds of English folklore, owls are considered useless, lazy and foolish in Hindi culture.

A mature business has systems and processes in place to make sure everything runs smoothly and, if things go wrong, they can be easily put back on the right track. It's not necessarily easy, which is why having an understanding of which assets are important to a business, thanks to Daniel Priestley's book, helped a great deal.

One of the hardest assets for GoLocalise to manage successfully was our sales and marketing pipeline. You can have the best business in the world but if you don't have enough customers lined up or your sales pipeline is not big enough, things are going to be difficult. In our case, we were confident we had the best translators, the best voice talent and the best systems in place, but we always worried about having enough work. Without jobs coming in, it would be hard to move forward.

Remember I issued a spoiler alert a few pages back? The future of my business, as with everyone else's, was thrown into question by global events in 2020–2021. The pandemic was, in terms of GoLocalise sales, an especially difficult time. On a personal note, I was managing the business alone in a London apartment during the long periods of lockdown. My new husband and beloved pet dog, Rambo, who had been my constant companion since he was six weeks old, were on the other side of the Atlantic. Isolation was tough and it all felt a long way from the highly supportive, busy office environment I was used to. The situation is possibly best described as running in panic mode because we didn't know what was going to happen or how long any of it would last.

A big problem was that the supply of content dried up. As a business, GoLocalise depends on a steady stream of new material in English to translate and adapt (localise) into foreign languages and markets. If new content is not being created, there is unfortunately little for us to do. This immediately forced me to make some tough decisions and we said goodbye to some valued colleagues through no fault of their own. Knowing that we were working towards a greater good – keeping the business afloat – did not make those moments any easier.

With production stopped because film crews couldn't physically be together, we set about trying to win work with our skeleton staff. We contacted clients and proposed creative solutions for animation or repurposing existing content. We tried lots of things, but it was difficult to make headway. To complicate matters, the decision-makers our team would normally talk to, of course, were all working from home too and dealing with their own lockdowns. We couldn't go and see them. Many were furloughed themselves and so we often found ourselves needing to pick up conversations with people we didn't know, which proved difficult. Even when we spoke to clients, their budgets and schedules became meaningless as nobody knew how long production would be at a standstill. It was a difficult situation for everyone: everything was up in the air, nobody could plan anything and we couldn't compare it to anything that had gone before. I know our small team often felt overwhelmed during this period, but we put our best foot forward. Our only response was to go into overdrive, to keep going step by step, playing things by ear and trying new creative strategies to try and ride out the storm.

In hindsight, I'm honestly not sure how we managed but I am proud, ultimately, of what we achieved at GoLocalise during the lockdown period. We did more than survive; we learned a lot about who we were and what we could deliver when it mattered.

There was a glimmer of hope things might start to return to normal in November 2021, only for the Omicron variant to throw a spanner in the works again before that Christmas. By the following summer, people were just about overcoming their fears and slowly returning to work. Work, however, did not immediately slot back into place. In fact, as I write this, you could argue it still hasn't. We've been hit by one event after another. There is a war between Ukraine and Russia, and to top it off we are also in the middle of a cost-of-living crisis. There has been a revolving door at Number 10 Downing Street and, if we're being honest about politics, we are probably still feeling the full effects of Brexit. There hasn't been time for any of us to draw breath and, as a result, we're all still feeling dazed, confused and, frankly, exhausted.

Thinking of GoLocalise today, as I write this in March 2023, this constant uncertainty means persuading our clients to spend money with us is still a challenge.

We think, as you might imagine, localising content is essential but for many of our clients it is an extra service. They might say, 'We already have our campaign in English. Do we really need it in another language?' The answer sometimes varies between a maybe and a flat no. As a result, our services get cut back or dropped entirely if money is tight.

Aware of this, we started to think differently about the process of winning work. As we coped with the impact of lockdown, we started analysing our sales pipeline through a new lens with the help of Martin Norbury, who you previously met in Chapter 7. Since starting the business, I had always been fortunate enough to enjoy a healthy number of inbound enquiries. We became good at responding with the right answers, winning projects and delivering high-quality work. This is the bulletproof way, after all. Clients would come back to us time after time, which put us in the comfortable position of having regular customers. At one point, almost half of our turnover came from just one. This was great until the day that one client stopped using us. It wasn't because we had delivered a bad job, become too expensive or any other reason under our control. They simply lost a major client themselves and their localisation requirements, viewed as no longer essential, fizzled out. Having learned a lesson about having all our eggs in one basket (you can read more about this in Chapter 9) we set about changing the profile of our client base. In our early days, 80% of our turnover was split between just four clients. Once we'd completed our analysis and work with Martin, the same 80% was split between twenty-five. With a diverse client base (or more eggs in more baskets) we aren't so badly affected if we lose one or two of them along the way.

Winning more clients, of course, didn't just happen. It meant shifting to a proactive state of mind and getting on the front foot. We made sure everyone in GoLocalise put part of their day aside, often a few hours in the morning, to make direct contact with a target list of organisations we might want to work with. I say everyone, but we quickly learned sales wasn't a role that came naturally to the entire team. People tend to split into two clear categories. There are team members who enjoy client-facing work, and they embraced the challenge of making new business contacts enthusiastically. There are also team members who definitely do not enjoy that kind of work. Typically, they are diligent and productive worker bees, and asking them to become more like butterflies flitting between phone calls, meetings and presentations made these people miserable, which we didn't want. Eventually, however, once we had allocated the work to the right people, we reached a happy place where proactive sales effort was embedded within the GoLocalise operation and culture.

Extra effort doesn't automatically equal better results, of course. Our problem, familiar to many salespeople I'm sure, was speaking to the right people. Emails were unanswered and phone messages were rarely returned. Even old-school snail mail failed to make an impact. Gatekeepers, it seemed, blocked our every move. To solve this problem, we played to our new-found strengths and set about the task creatively.

We have run many marketing campaigns in recent years, but I think I'll share my favourite because it embodies our quirky inventive spirit. We bought dozens of old-school Nokia phones that anyone from the nineties would recognise, complete with the Snake game and those iconic ringtones. We sent them in beautiful eye-catching red boxes along with out-of-the-ordinary sales letters. We sent the packages by special delivery too, as they needed to be signed for and we would know when they had arrived. Our targets were a bunch of ideal clients we had previously researched and so we knew we wanted to work with them. We assumed, rightly it turns out, that an actual physical parcel in these days of e-communication would get noticed and opened. Once we had proof of delivery, we would ring the mobile phone inside the box and, in a stroke, have a conversation with the person we wanted. Who wouldn't pick up a mysterious phone when it rang? A couple of our targets said yes and we won enough work to make a return on the investment that had made the campaign happen. Even when the response was a polite 'no thank you' we, at least, gained something. People appreciated our sense of humour and the effort we had gone to. They would remember the GoLocalise name if we contacted them in the future. Thinking outside the box and putting a phone in a box worked for us.

Thanks to this shift to thinking proactively and creatively about sales and marketing, we are more confident than ever that we are speaking to the right people and know what jobs are on the horizon. We can now act at the right time rather than in the panic-induced reactive ways of the recent past. This is another example of the constant reinvention that is required when you own and run a business.

> **LESSON: Don't settle for second best, continually evolve and re-invent yourself**
>
> You don't have to be a huge fan of her music to recognise Madonna as the queen of reinvention. She has been in business for over forty years, sold millions of records and has, without question, enjoyed a bulletproof career. Originally a singer from the New York City club scene, she was signed in the early 1980s having hustled hard to promote her first single on both sides of the Atlantic. Her synth-based disco proved irresistible, and her first album was a five-times platinum disc winner. For her second album, *Like a Virgin*, she used her new fame to hire a world-class producer, Chic's Nile Rodgers, and the hits kept coming. In her third album she consciously moved away from pop to a richer, denser sound which included classical arrangements. The songs were more thoughtful too and tackled societal issues including, in the case of 'Papa Don't Preach', teenage pregnancy. For her fourth album, she turned to her religious upbringing and Latin American roots for inspiration. After the release of *Like A Prayer* she went on her Blond Ambition World Tour, which became a cultural phenomenon with memorable

> costumes from Jean Paul Gaultier. It made Madonna the second-highest-earning musician at the time behind Michael Jackson. Today, she has produced fourteen studio albums, sold a total of 300 million units and been recognised as the world's top-selling artist by Guinness World Records. At the time of writing, her planned Celebration Tour, marking her sixty-fourth birthday, is selling out all over the world. She owes this success to a relentless march forward and constant search for new ways to express herself.
>
> We don't all want to be Madonna, but I do think there's a lesson to learn from her and all music acts that grab and engage their audiences over time. By constantly changing, they can stay in the charts for decades producing single after single, album after album and tour after tour. It's the same with business: one-hit wonders come and go, but inventive and flexible organisations stay relevant in their industries for decades.

I would hate you to think that I advocate the rock-and-roll lifestyle, mind you. These days, I hate the idea of life on the road, and I much prefer to travel at a relaxed pace purely for pleasure. I don't want a gruelling schedule of long hours to get in the way of spending time with friends and family either. I know I am not alone. The Covid-19 pandemic made many of us take a fresh look at our work–life balance.

What has the changing attitude towards work meant to GoLocalise? We have certainly re-assessed the way we think about productivity. It is easy, sometimes, to measure effort and commitment by who stayed late or who worked over the weekend. Now, as a boss, I am much less interested in who is in the office and how long they stay. If one of my team does a fantastic job in less time than we expected, for example, I feel it's important to celebrate that win and not worry too much about what they do for the rest of the day. I know it's not practical for all businesses, but my main observation is that as long as work gets done and everyone can be trusted to deliver to the required quality, micromanaging colleagues' schedules is unhelpful and feels a practice best left in the past. I want to spend more of my time with family and my husband enjoying nice restaurants and walking our dog. Why wouldn't I offer the same opportunities and freedoms to my team?

In exploring these ideas, I have learned a lot about my co-workers. I have concluded there are two different types of people in both GoLocalise and the world in general. As an individual, your response to work falls into one of two clear camps. You may respond to any task you are given methodically like an ant. This is not a bad thing. Ants achieve incredible things. They clear forests, move mountains and build huge colonies, but always with a plan. They work calmly one step at a time without making a fuss. If you recognise yourself, congratulations. Ants are amazing to have on your team. We love ants.

Mayflies, on the other hand, get things done quickly because they never have enough time. They buzz in, dart around and create amazing infectious energy.

They get things done at the last minute because they know they operate best at speed. If you are a mayfly, relax. We love mayflies too. Your ants will meticulously work to schedule and plan a balanced relationship between work and home life. Your mayflies might be less organised, but they'll bring their energy and enthusiasm when you need it.

As I'm writing this, we are working on a hybrid policy for GoLocalise to keep both camps happy. We're planning a three-month trial of flexible working. I have concerns because we have a lot of junior people to consider, and I think they often need support and coaching which requires managers to be onsite with them. I certainly did when I started my career. Breaking things down and explaining tasks one-to-one is invaluable. We're not sceptical about remote work, but we just want to see what works best for everyone at every level of the business. Change is always a process of trial and error. We're staying flexible.

Again, my shifting personal priorities have played a significant role here too. I certainly hadn't planned to move to the USA when I was in my twenties, but here I am – a married man writing this from my sunny desk in our place in Fort Lauderdale, South Florida.

While we're chatting about the process of change, it's worth saying that I wish this book had more of a traditional narrative about life and love. I would have dearly loved to tell you how I set myself clear relationship goals, and perhaps shared, step by step, how I went about finding happiness. That, however, would not be entirely honest of me. The only insight I can share 100% truthfully is the fact that I embraced the wonderful nature of serendipity and good fortune when it came my way. When, in 2018, I happened to go on a Caribbean cruise, I did not expect to meet and start dating someone who lived on the other side of the Atlantic Ocean, in Puerto Rico to be precise – but that's exactly what happened.

Aaron and I obviously hit it off and got on well quickly. He came to visit, met my family, attended a couple of weddings with me and soon felt part of the family. Mind you, after months of flying back and forth to Puerto Rico I was, frankly, knackered, and it was also expensive. After nine months or so, we agreed that staying put and continuing a long-distance relationship wasn't a great idea. There was no ultimatum or anything like that. I had spent time visiting Puerto Rico and Aaron had stayed with me in London and, because that felt so good, creating a home together seemed the obvious next step for both of us. Where we lived was the only question and fate played a hand here too. Aaron had worked for a TV channel in Puerto Rico for many years and, thanks to his long service, was entitled to a year's sabbatical. He had always wanted to improve his English and experience living in Europe. The answer was for him to take a year off and come to live with me in London.

The first thing that happened when we got settled in the UK was, of course, Aaron getting sick. I've written about my cheeky but lovable dog, Rambo, earlier in the book. Anyone who loves dogs knows how entwined they become in our stories. By this point Rambo had, fortunately, bonded beautifully with Aaron. They quickly became wonderful friends. This meant we became a family unit. The three of us, looking after each other.

Walking Rambo around the green spaces of London became part of Aaron's routine. He liked it. He still felt like a tourist and London's sights and sounds were exciting for him to explore. Less exciting to explore was the London weather. He would often go out on cold winter evenings. As he was from the Caribbean, he thought nothing of wearing tank tops, flip-flops and little shorts. He wanted to feel cute and sexy, right? He was amazed that everyone wore so many clothes in London and wrapped themselves up so tightly – so boring. That was, of course, until he caught a stinking cold. More than one. It seemed to go on for ages. Although I'd warned him, he chose not to believe me until he had fully experienced feeling snottily miserable for himself.

Later, of course, while experiencing Chinatown in London's glittering West End, he spotted women on loud giggly nights out letting their hair down in sandals and minidresses. I remember his double take. Where were their coats? Why were they not wrapped up in scarves and bobble hats? Who wears strappy tops when it is minus two degrees? I had to explain to my husband, a new visitor to Britain's shores, that when it came to having a party in the UK, booze had strange and wonderful magical properties. Looking back, so many lessons about English life made us both chuckle in those days.

WORDS: Translation interlude

The English have a wonderfully broad vocabulary when talking about drunkenness. You can be 'three sheets to the wind', 'drunk as a skunk', 'plastered', 'smashed', 'tipsy', 'well-oiled', 'legless', 'sloshed' and 'sozzled'. English, however, doesn't have a monopoly on creative ways to describe a state of inebriation. In Spanish, you can be 'boiled' (*Ir cocido*) or, less charmingly perhaps, 'a fart' (*estar pédo*). In French, a drunk person could be 'a wine bag' (*un sac à vin*) or 'a pillar of the bar' (*un pilier du bar*). They might be 'buttered' (*beurré*), 'soaked' (*imbibé*), 'black' (*noir*), 'grey' (*gris*) or just 'gone' (*parti*). Looking further afield, Cantonese speakers don't binge-drink, they 'chop' or 'split' alcohol (*Pī jiǔ* / 劈酒). Chop too much booze and you might 'become a cat' (*Biànchéng yī zhī māo* / 變成一隻貓).

There wasn't much partying once Aaron moved to London. We quickly settled into a routine. I worked and Aaron went to English school during the day. He was used to Netflix and American films so when he came to England he struggled to understand the differences between the British and the American cultures. Not just language, but accents, attitudes and behaviours too. I have been in England since the late nineties. After living in Britain for twenty-plus years,

I have become accustomed to many things that English people do – I guess I 'got localised' without even realising, pardon the pun. Whether you want to or not, you become like a sponge. For instance, Brits tend to be super polite and say sorry a lot. If you bump into a British person on the street or catch their heel with your supermarket trolley, they will immediately apologise for getting in your way. It's blatantly not their fault, but they feel compelled to apologise for taking up space.

Talking of supermarkets, Aaron would often comment that I got angry when out shopping. I initially denied this, but soon realised I was quietly seething at anyone who was impolite and didn't say please or thank you. How dare they? Without question, this is something I've learned by living in Britain. Aaron, having lived in the USA and in the Caribbean, cares less about such niceties. He doesn't want people to be actively rude, of course, but is more likely to judge people on their actions and intentions than their Ps and Qs. Whereas I, because I now know the unspoken rules of engagement, get upset if I hear them broken even from a distance across grocery aisles.

Aaron is also perplexed by the way British people, or perhaps more accurately the English, say yes or no. Transactions are undertaken in a code it can take a lifetime to decipher. 'That sounds interesting' means the precise opposite and is a firm no, for example. 'Oh, you must come for dinner' is a warm, kind invitation in any other culture. For the English, it's a total brush-off and you will never see those people again. Arranging any kind of event or activity with locals in London seems to need such an exhausting level of linguistic analysis for immigrants, it is a wonder the city functions at all.

This brings the discussion back to how I've changed and evolved living in a culture that is not my own. It is an issue I have based my working life on exploring. Localisation and adapting content from one market to another is fascinating. It's more than translating words. English is spoken in Singapore, America, Ireland, England, Scotland and Wales, for example, but is experienced differently in each of those places. I'm aware, of course, that Aaron and I and our transatlantic relationship provide an example of localisation in practice. Today, we're a European–Caribbean couple living in the USA. Previously we were living in London. You can imagine it has taken a little while for us to feel at home anywhere.

Localisation, of the type I deliver through GoLocalise, is about making organisations feel at home and their products and services feel familiar, not only in different languages but in different cultures too. If you're British, think about the relationship you have with the US culture. You may recognise parts of it because American films, TV and music dominate our airwaves. You may, as a result, be able to watch baseball and recognise a home run when you see one; however, you're likely to be flummoxed by the detailed intricacies of the rules. Unlike a child who grew up in the States, you may never have played the game yourself. Similarly, when businesses begin to market across cultures, they frequently encounter linguistic problems. Translating product and company names can be difficult; translating advertising slogans can be downright impossible. Over the years, some of the largest and most marketing-savvy companies have made some of the biggest translation blunders.

WORDS: Translation interlude

Translating English brand names or slogans into Asian languages can be particularly difficult. When you choose the closest approximate sound to your brand name, the resulting word can have an undesirable meaning. As I mentioned in Chapter 4, when Coca-Cola was first translated phonetically into Chinese, the resultant phrase meant 'bite the wax tadpole'. Coke finally marketed its product under an alternate phrase, which sounded less like 'Coca-Cola' but carried the more appetising meaning 'can mouth, can happy'. KFC (formerly known as Kentucky Fried Chicken) found that its 'Finger-Lickin' Good' slogan was translated into Chinese as the admonition 'Eat Your Fingers Off'. Coca-Cola also had trouble in other markets. A few years ago, the jingle 'Have a Coke and a Smile' was translated into French. Although the translation was technically correct, words aren't always heard clearly when they're sung, and the song sounded like 'Have a Coke and a Mouse'. Sometimes mistranslations are caused by circumstances beyond anyone's control. The wind

> caused an unfortunate alteration of a Coke skywriting ad in Cuba. The ad was supposed to read '*Tome Coca-Cola*' ('Drink Coca-Cola'), but the wind blurred the second letter, making the message '*Teme Coca-Cola*' – 'Fear Coca-Cola'.
>
> Even when a translation is accurate, marketing can be undermined by local slang, dialect and seemingly random events. Basing quick translations of what you need on assumptions isn't true localisation. Even if you're a well-trained linguist, you can still be a world away from living, working and being embedded in the target country. It's not easy, but incredibly rewarding when you get it right.

Back to my story. Ultimately, it was always the plan to move to the USA with Aaron. I think when someone is from the Caribbean, they need the sun. You won't get them in Chicago, New York or London for long. While he was in London, Aaron got a job offer in Orlando, Florida and I decided to go with him. This meant, among other things, becoming a remote boss and running the office in London from across the pond. Today, I fly to the UK once a quarter and, of course, we have regular Zoom meetings. Despite being five hours behind on the clock, we have made an efficient routine work. I am less involved operationally, which has allowed my team to grow and develop and freed me up to steer the business from the front. I would never have expected such a turn of events when I started the business or, indeed, when I wrote the first edition of this book… but here we are.

Now I am looking at life from a different point of view and have been through experiences that have taught me a lot – not just business lessons, but life lessons too. In my case, the tough times of the pandemic, when running GoLocalise was difficult, are intrinsically linked with happier news around forming a life with Aaron and Rambo in a new country. It's impossible to separate the two experiences. Work and home life, as I suspect is the case for most business owners, come as one package.

Looking back on the period the book covers, I'm not sure I could or would have done anything differently. From a childhood of chorizo sandwiches in Spain when things were tough, through spending my young adult life in London to now settling in the USA, I've faced every day as an adventure. There have been periods when I've been scared it might have all come crashing down around my ears, but I've always persevered and I can tell you now, it has been worth every moment.

> **LESSON: Be comfortable, happy and content**
>
> If you think back to the early part of the book, for all the incidents I recount, you won't remember much about any burning ambition. Every class had at least one kid with blinkered vision steering them relentlessly down the path of being a police officer or a zookeeper. Well... that definitely wasn't me. Even as a teenager, although I loved radio, languages and communication, I didn't have a path plotted out for me. You could argue

> university and early employment were slight missteps. I have huge respect for the legal profession, but the law and I were never going to get on. I'm sure many around me, as I grew up, found this frustrating, but I didn't. When I look back, my sole ambition was to be comfortable, happy and content. That's what drove me then, and still does today. I fantasised about being a millionaire, yes, but not because of the money. As a child, I couldn't comprehend what a million pounds actually meant. All that appealed to me was the stress-free lifestyle and not having to worry about money. My point is if you have a child who seems to lack ambition (or you are one), relax. Not everybody needs laser-sharp focus on a specific plan. Living a complete, happy life is what is important. Running a business has, it turns out, allowed me to do that, for which I will always remain eternally grateful.

Talking of feeling complete, I am delighted to be spending less time working and more time with my partner and my family at this stage of my life. I own a mature business that is operating smoothly. My English customers might say it's all tickety boo. Any customers in Poland might think it's a roll with butter. I'm not planning to sell it, but I know more about what it is worth when that time comes. My new attitude reflects the fact that my priorities have changed. It feels different from when I started the business but… isn't that the point? For a business to count as a success, doesn't it have to change and adapt along with its owner? As I reflect on where I have come from, everything I've been through and where my life is today, I feel more bulletproof than ever.

Conclusion

You will have noticed throughout the pages of this book that certain phrases were written in bold type. These were the learning bullets which hold my story together – the ammunition which will help you to become bulletproof yourself. I have shared some of my own examples, but I'd encourage you to find things in your life where they ring true, then build on them and make each one stronger.

Let me recap the main points on how to become bulletproof in a nutshell.

You need money to live (you can read more about this in Chapter 2). I have nothing but admiration for altruistic people who seem to put others before themselves all of the time and spend their lives on missions to change the world, but selfless people are few and far between. No matter how much you like or dislike capitalism, it is impossible to survive without income in the modern world unless you have inherited millions, won the lottery or are so well situated that a good standard of living is guaranteed for your entire life. If so, good luck to you. You are in a position to do as you please each and every day.

All of us can do pretty much anything we please, as long as we ask ourselves the question, 'Can I make any money out of pursuing this course?' I urge you to think seriously about this when choosing your direction in life.

It is true that money isn't everything, nor can it bring you happiness, but not having it can certainly bring unhappiness to a good person trying to do the right thing. I am not promoting greed; I am saying that money is not a dirty word. You can read how, after all my trials and tribulations, I've reached a comfortable stage in life thanks to money in Chapter 11.

Love it before you can earn from it (you can read more about this in Chapter 3). Having established that your passion is a viable commercial opportunity, you can put the thought of finance aside for a while (once you have worked out your numbers and made sure the finances add up) and let your love for what you are doing take over. While earning an income is important, enjoying what you do and getting a sense of achievement will always be a bigger motivator.

I know a few people who are motivated purely by money, but in my experience, they are rare (and, to be honest, not particularly personable). Most people I know, and all of the successful (and bulletproof) ones, are passionate about the business or life path that they have chosen to pursue.

It is never too late to make a change (you can read more about this in Chapter 3). Have you ever heard the expression 'being stuck in a rut'? It will come as no surprise that it is an easily translatable one because it is a disease that plagues people in most modern societies. When you are young, it is difficult to decide what you want to do with the rest of your life. The concept of adult responsibility seems so far away and there is still exploring to be done and adventure to discover, but in my opinion, that is how people end up in the rut in the first place.

When it comes to doing work, strength comes from aiming to **do a perfect job** (you can read more about this in Chapter 4). In many ways, this is what the entire book is about. I am a realist, and I know that perfection is a rare commodity indeed. Maybe it is impossible (and overrated) to be perfect in what you do, or maybe perfection is too time-consuming to be worth the effort and reward – there are certain businesses, or areas within them, where seeking perfection can be detrimental to the bigger picture, but I also know it stands out when it happens.

My good friend Nigel Botterill says, 'The average piece of marketing that gets sent is better than the perfect piece that never gets sent', and he is absolutely right. The fact remains that perfection stands out from the average, and in the exact world of translation and localisation there is nothing that will build your reputation, your work supply and the rates that you can charge more than perfection. This must apply to many other businesses and walks of life too.

You have to **believe in yourself** (you can read more about this in Chapter 5). Belief is an interesting concept, and a powerful one. It would perhaps sound oversimplistic of me to say that those with self-belief invariably perform better than those without, but it is true. I realise that believing in yourself takes more than just me telling you that you need to – I am not a psychologist or motivational speaker with a gift for imparting self-belief, but I do know that it helps.

If I can tie it back to the idea of being bulletproof, then hopefully I can give you something of value to take away about self-belief. Whenever you do some work, submit a proposal or have a go at something new, an inner voice will tell you whether you gave it your all. Before you press the 'go' button, why not listen to that voice and see if you could have done better? If you believe that you have done the task to the best of your ability, why shouldn't you believe that it is fantastic, or at the least, good enough?

You can only do your best, and if you do that you will always get better results than if you gave 80%. Better results lead to more confidence the next time, and more confidence leads to better results the time after that. Soon you'll be so full of belief that you might even make it to being bulletproof.

My next tip is to surround yourself with talented, honest and direct people. **Being flawless and becoming bulletproof** means working with the best (you can read more about this in Chapter 7). Tell me who you hang around with, and I will tell you who you will become. If you can hug friendly dogs once in a while, that's probably good for you too. The people who are useful at the start of your career are a great asset, so keep them close. They'll grow with you as you **keep going to infinity and beyond** (see Chapter 7).

As you and your business mature, it is normal to find you need different people in your life – keep looking. **Be adaptable when necessary and specific if required** (again, you can read about this in Chapter 7), because the world is always changing, and if you want to be successful you have to change with it. Being set stubbornly in your ways is not a good strategy for getting on in a world ruled by change. In many cases, particularly in marketing, what was a good idea last year may not be effective today. The Yellow Pages used to be the place to be seen, but today they are hardly seen at all. Spamming by email worked once upon a time, but when a million people were doing it, the market had had enough. Who, in a thousand years, could have imagined TikTok today? The march is relentlessly forward.

My best advice when dealing with change is to watch the leaders in your marketplace (or other marketplaces if appropriate) and see what they are doing. There are a lot of smart people in business today and they are the ones to learn from and imitate. A great example is Google's purchase of YouTube for US$1.65bn back in 2008. Analysts called them reckless. The world was up in arms. By 2021 Google was making US$1.65bn in revenue from YouTube every three weeks. Name a better acquisition.

Life doesn't always go to plan, of course. Sometimes, **change can hit you in the face**. Part of the reason I revised this book is to share the lessons I learned through the pandemic. Being away from my partner, locked alone in an apartment and running a business through a massive economic downturn was probably the toughest period of my life. I got through and that has built confidence that I will get through other, maybe bigger, challenges to come. The lesson here is that you never need to panic or assume the worst. When you are facing the greatest challenges, you will be at your strongest.

During tough times, it's worth remembering that **your business works like an engineering problem**

(Chapter 7) with its own cogs, wheels, levers, conveyor belts and inputs and outputs. By viewing GoLocalise in this dispassionate way, thanks to the coaching and support of Martin Norbury, I planned our response to the Covid-19 pandemic and built new and improved sales processes. Not all my decisions paid off, of course. It is inevitable, as a business owner, you are going to take wrong turns and mess things up once in a while. The best response to mistakes is, of course, to learn from them. If you can say, and mean, **never again** when something goes awry, then you'll continually improve (you can read more about this in Chapter 9). As human beings, we have continually proved we are a resilient species and can bounce back from pretty much anything.

Throughout our ups and downs, many of us deny the passing of the years but there is no getting away from age. Embracing it can mean whatever you want it to mean but it does mean shifting priorities. If you're a business owner, that means **getting your business sales-ready** (you can read more about that in Chapter 11). Without a plan for the future, I wouldn't be married now. I wouldn't be living in Fort Lauderdale, Florida. I would still be working 24/7 without time to enjoy the slower, more family focused life I enjoy now.

In the West, generally speaking, we are far more fortunate than many in the world, and we have a choice in what we do with our lives. We can make a difference to our circumstances by thinking more clearly, having bigger dreams, acting more smartly and being bolder, but far too many people don't take hold of the opportunities and the possibilities that surround them. Because our nature is to put up with it, the easy option is always to do just that. I'm suggesting real success comes from **never settling for second best and continually evolving** as a person and a business owner. Why not adopt the British Bulldog spirit (I won't attempt to translate that) which says 'I will not give in'? The greatest attributes of the success-driven bulletproof person are that they're determined to make changes and be the best they can be.

These ideas are the bullets that you can use to fire up your route to being bulletproof.

And finally:

I speak to a lot of students studying language at university, presumably with a view to going into some sort of linguistic career. Originally, I wanted to write this book as an encouragement to them, sharing some of my experiences and the lessons I have learned in my journey so far, but as I assembled my thoughts, I realised that there might be a far wider group of people I could help. This is certainly true of this second edition. Whether you are studying for a master's degree in translation, working as a freelance linguist, a new business owner, an experienced entrepreneur, starting a business in another country, working for someone else and dreaming about doing your own thing, or pursuing any other course in life, this book is my encouragement to you.

If you apply time, effort and positive thought to becoming bulletproof, it will make you a better version of yourself in life and business. The best version of you will be better off financially, happier, more fulfilled, respected among those you care about, and able to pass on your expertise to others. All it takes is application and effort.

It is true that some people are born with a silver spoon in their mouth, and others might just be more naturally gifted in a particular area, but everyone can grow to become bulletproof. Whatever your circumstances are today, you can do better, achieve more and be happier as a result. In my experience, the result is worth far more than the effort you put in.

Acknowledgements

This book would not have been possible without the support and encouragement of many people at different points in my life.

I have to first thank my family for being there for me through thick and thin. My mum has been my rock and I will always be grateful to my grandparents for my upbringing and for instilling in me important life values. I wish to thank my auntie Sara for encouraging me to follow my dreams and providing support along the way. I also want to acknowledge my entire family for their love and support, particularly during my childhood and teenage years when I was an uncontrollable devil.

I want to give a huge thanks to the Entrepreneurs Circle staff and its members, especially Nigel Botterill who was my Mastermind mentor and whom I admire and respect greatly. Something lit up in me and he made me think like an entrepreneur.

I am truly grateful to Martin Norbury, who is a strong scalability coach, and to Jacki Norbury and the entire Advocate team. Few people have had the impact that they had on me through their amazing support, encouragement and tremendous positive energy and processes.

One of my true inspirations has been Professor Jorge Díaz-Cintas when it comes to translation and linguistics, and being a supportive friend. The area of audiovisual translation would not be the same without his extensive knowledge and contributions through research.

I also wish to acknowledge Stewart Dickison, my former manager at Technicolor and dear friend who taught me a lot about the translation market and gave me the tools essential to my own business.

The book would not be the same without Arani Chatterjee's humorous illustrations that helped bring it to life.

Special mention must be given to Martin Gladdish, my book coach, for his valuable input and advice.

ACKNOWLEDGEMENTS

Words cannot express my gratitude to Lucy McCarraher and the Rethink Press team for their professional advice and assistance in polishing this manuscript.

Lastly, I cannot forget to thank my friends for helping me brainstorm, for giving their honest feedback and for reading the manuscript. No matter how successful one becomes in business, nothing can beat great friends in life.

The Author

Spanish-born David García González is an English and Spanish audiovisual translator turned multi-award-winning entrepreneur and business owner. He has been based in London for over twenty years.

David runs GoLocalise, a localisation company specialising in the audiovisual field (translation, subtitling and voice-overs). Under David's leadership, GoLocalise grew three-fold and achieved international recognition by winning Outstanding Business in the Global Business Excellence Awards and Best Product/Service Range in the Best Business Awards in 2015.

David has won a multitude of awards, including: National Entrepreneur of the Month May 2015, Outstanding Entrepreneur in both Global Business Excellence Awards and Best Business Awards 2015, Most Inspiring Member Entrepreneurs Circle 2015, and finalist for the Entrepreneur of the Year 2015.

His previous job experience includes working as a radio presenter, voice-over talent (Discovery Channel, Nickelodeon and Cartoon Network and even the voice of the Paco Rabanne fragrances) and audiovisual translator and language director.

He received his BA Hons degree in TEFL and computer applications from Essex University and two MA degrees, one in applied translation studies from London Metropolitan University and the second in audiovisual translation at UAB.

He currently speaks at events, conferences and universities in the UK and overseas, drawing from personal experiences. His talks tackle the existing gap between being a linguist and an entrepreneur, as well as how to stand out from the crowd and land a job in a highly competitive industry. Showing how to build these bridges in a practical and easy-to-apply way is his blueprint, which takes him back to his Boy Scout days in his childhood.

David enjoys sharing his knowledge and business sense with his fellow translators and entrepreneurs

THE AUTHOR

both online and offline. He helps businesses of all sizes communicate their messages effectively in over 100 languages.

To find out more about David's work, go to his website:

🌐 www.davidgarciagonzalez.com